MW01628358

INTERNATIONAL

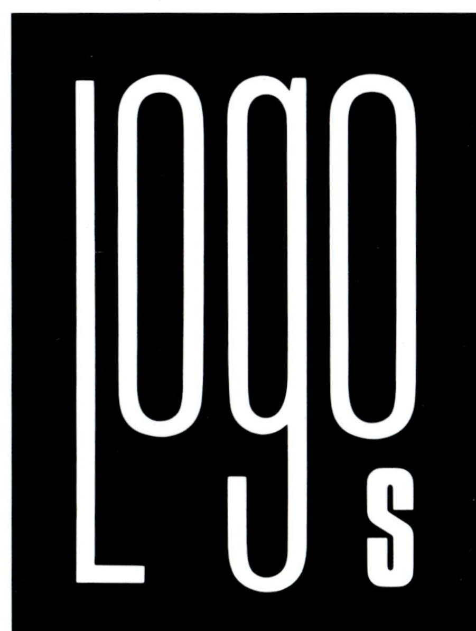

While Supon Design Group makes every effort possible to publish full and correct credits for each work included in this volume, sometimes errors of omission or commission may occur. For this we are most regretful, but hereby must disclaim any liability.

As this book is printed in four-color process, a few of the designs reproduced here may appear to be slightly different than in their original reproduction.

ISBN 8230-6093-4
Library of Congress Catalog
Card Number 90-063735

Distributors to the trade in the United States and Canada:
Watson-Guptill Publications
1515 Broadway
New York, NY 10036

Distributed throughout the rest of the world by:
Hearst Books International
105 Madison Avenue
New York, NY 10016

Publisher:
Madison Square Press
10 East 23rd Street
New York, NY 10010

Washington Trademark Design Competition is a Project of:
Supon Design Group, Inc.
2033 M Street, NW, Suite 801
Washington, DC 20036

Printed in Hong Kong

Winners from the International Logos and Trademarks of the 1980's Competition

Sponsored by Washington Trademark Design

WASHINGTON TRADEMARK DESIGN'S
International Logos & Trademarks of the 1980's

Project Director
Supon Phornirunlit

Communications Director
Wayne Kurie

Judges
Keith Bright
Joel Fuller
Julia LaPine
Rex Peteet
Valerie Richardson
Pat Taylor

Art Director
Supon Phornirunlit

Concept Designer
Jeffrey S. Dale

Book Designer
Dianne S. Cook

Photographer
Oi Jakrarat Veerasarn

Assistant Writer
Linda Klinger

Support Staff
Kimber Bennett
Nelton E. Castro
John Coleman
Andrew Dolan
Stephanie Hooton
Yang S. Kim
Jennifer Lowe
Robert Michael
Brett Nation
John Ng
Supranee Ng
Tony Wilkerson

Technical Support
TJ Consultants

A very special thank you to:
Jill Bossert
Elayne Brink
Kelly Crossley
Frank Parsons Paper Company, Inc.
The Graphic Artist's Book Club
Todd Green
Gerald McConnell

CONTENTS

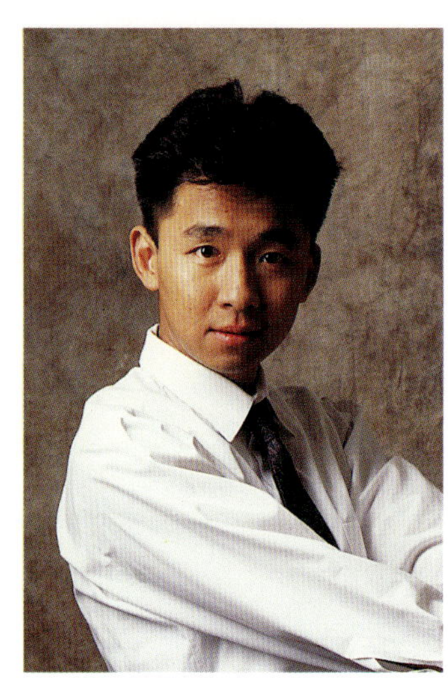

Supon Phornirunlit

What makes for a good logo? A lot of things in a small package. Simplicity and interest, to start. It must have style, proportion. It must communicate and support the company image. Be appropriate. And it must be unique. Keith Bright, of Bright & Associates, asserts, "A good logo makes me feel good." Rex Peteet, of Sibley/Peteet Design, says, "It must capture the lowest common denominator." And Joel Fuller, of Pinkhaus Design: "There's no in-between—it's either good or bad."

This year, Washington Trademark Design sponsored its second competition. We received thousands of entries from around the world. Included herein are those logos and trademarks that not only made outstanding first impressions, but lasting impressions as well. We are honoring them so that excellence can be better understood, recognized, and rewarded.

How many times have I waded through the river of brochures and corporate identity pieces that flow in with the daily mail, always picking out the piece that makes a powerful statement, and sweeping the rest into the trash? Or, when in a supermarket and faced with shelves of choices, why do I always buy the product with the unique logo on its package? And how often am I disappointed when what's inside doesn't match the quality of what's outside?

An important concept underscores both brochures and canned foods. Some companies understand the need for good product or corporate representation—that all-important first impression. And many other organizations (sometimes those with the better product) do not understand this at all.

Pat Taylor, of Pat Taylor, Inc., says that a trademark distinguishes its namesake by associating itself with a characteristic of the company. It's a link to the origin of the product or service. Not only is a logo often the public's first contact with an organization, sometimes a prospective client will look no further than at this and the product description, when making a choice. A logo must tell as much as possible about the product and organization it represents. It can't just look good—it must also communicate well.

Of the thousands of entries received, hundreds had the same concept. In some cases, they even looked alike, even though they may have come from different countries. We did see cliches (symbols, such as eagles, stars, pencils, hearts, hands, crosses), but there were always a few excellent marks by designers who treated these images in a refreshing way.

"One direction seems to be the moving away from abstract geometric solutions to more stylized, tangible symbols," says Peteet. "Many are rediscovering type and being very playful. Surprisingly, we saw numerous very detailed logo solutions that worked well. This could be another trend in response to the ultra-styled geometric marks of recent popularity."

Hornall Anderson Design Works' Julia LaPine agrees, "There is a wonderful movement toward warmer, more tangible imagery, as opposed to abstract and impersonal."

But establishing a trend, which is an accomplishment only apparent in retrospect, is a tricky business. Working within the evolution of new direction is effective only if the designer's trademark survives the trend's demise. Many trendy logos were entered into the competition, and most were ideas we'd already seen. Conversely, the trademarks in this book that were designed in the early 1980s—without following trends—still appear current.

"The best logos are timeless," LaPine concurs. "Viewing so many trademarks in a condensed amount of time tended to flush trends out rapidly. The same technique, shape, line, etc., applied over and over again, wore pretty thin." Valerie Richardson, of Richardson or Richardson: "Anything that seemed dependent upon a trend was generally not among the best work."

In sponsoring this competition, we were most excited at the international response. Winners came from 21 countries. It was enlightening to study these designs and try to understand the products, cultures, and languages associated with them. Fuller noted an example, "The Russian entries made you think: They were very abstract, deeper, on a different level." In retrospect, we learned more about our own lifestyles by viewing those represented by foreign entries.

We present the works in this book as our tribute to the designers who created them. They have set the standards for the industry with the very best in international communication arts of the last decade.
I congratulate them all, and hope readers will benefit from viewing their works. I also hope that this inspires designers to tap new intuitive resources that reside within all creative people.
Until then...

Born in Bangkok, Supon Phornirunlit studied design in Thailand, Japan, and the United States. He is now owner and Art Director of Supon Design Group, Inc., a graphic design studio formed in 1988. Currently, Supon is on the board of directors of the Art Directors Club of Metropolitan Washington and is Project Director of Washington Trademark Design. He and his studio are featured in the Washington journal of AIGA and in HOW*'s* 1990 Business Annual. *In the past two years, he has earned over fifty awards from organizations such as AIGA, the Art Directors Clubs of both New York and Washington, Type Directors Club, American Corporate Identity, DESI; as well as recognition in* Print's Design Annual. *The firm's corporate identity work has been exhibited in Bangkok, Germany, Japan, and Jerusalem.*

Wayne Kurie

The components that constitute success are always hard to define, but success itself is easy to recognize. There's no doubt that this year's Washington Trademark Design competition was a milestone event for everyone with an interest in graphic arts. As its Communications Director, I know that the most vital ingredient to WTD II's success was the people involved, and to them, I extend my sincere appreciation.

These people include our six judges: Keith Bright, Joel Fuller, Julia LaPine, Rex Peteet, Valerie Richardson, and Pat Taylor—you were great! And to our joint staffs here at Supon Design Group's Book Division and Washington Trademark Design II, thank you for your long, late hours and weekends of work. To our many assistants on judging days, thank you for volunteering your time. I must also acknowledge the thoughtfulness of editors, publishers, communications and public relations people worldwide who, at my modest request, publicized the competition in their newsletters, magazines, and flyers and on company bulletin boards, etc. Your enthusiasm brought even more excitement to the project.

But, most of all, my thanks go out to designers all over the world who submitted their work. Of course, we couldn't have done it without you. Indeed, we received almost 7,000 entries—many times what we had expected—from addresses that read like a world atlas. These entries represented a total of 31 countries and five continents. Just imagine the mountains of mail delivered to us daily, and the endless hours spent sorting and organizing the entries for the judges.

The weekend for judging had long been set for July 13-16, 1990. As is always the case, these dates arrived too quickly. And because of the enormous quantities of entries received just days before judging, it became clear that we would have to simplify our judging process. Gone were our original plans of scoring each piece, adding points, and selecting the highest scoring entries in each category. Instead, after an eleventh-hour meeting with the judges, we decided upon the following procedure.

On Day One of the two days of judging, we assigned six judges and seven staff assistants to one of two rooms, three judges in each. In both rooms, simultaneously, the assistants took turns showing each entry to the judges, one at a time. Information regarding the entry's year of production, country of origin, or nature of the client's business was available to the judges; the name of the designer or design firm was not. The judges then gave each entry a "yes" or "no" vote (in or out of the book). Any entry receiving three "no's" was discarded. If it received two or more "yes's," it was automatically entered. And any piece receiving only one "yes" was considered a "maybe" and kept for further discussion the next day.

On Day Two, the entries awarded with two or more "yes's" (approximately 500 total) were displayed on a table for all six judges to review. This was the day of deep thinking, pointed discussion and wrenching decisions, for we allowed each judge veto power over any piece that they strongly felt did not merit a place in our book. Strong feelings—that's what we wanted, and that's what we got!

...and so it went, until the 500 pieces were whittled down to a very competitive 351—those you see in this book.

"These winning entries are a strong record of what was accomplished in the last ten years," Richardson stated with satisfaction after the judging. And I think she summed up the way we all felt. So there you are—the best international logos and trademarks of the 1980s!

WTD II taught me a great deal about our industry. I thank all involved for giving me the opportunity to discover this wealth of original design. For more information on upcoming shows, events, and competitions, please mail the enclosed postcard. We all look forward to seeing more award-winning work at our next event. Meanwhile, I hope you can learn from the works which follow.

Wayne Kurie is Marketing and Sales Manager at Supon Design Group, Inc. He earned a Bachelor of Arts degree in marketing management from the University of Hartford and then went on to complete his MBA in international business at The George Washington University in Washington, DC. He began his career in marketing of design at the Washington Design Center and is now Communications Director of Washington Trademark Design. He has received awards recognizing his work from Creativity, *the Art Directors Club of Metropolitan Washington, and others.*

"Since most of the entries were so very well done, professional, and exciting, it was impossible to pick a single, really big winner."

Keith Bright

Bright & Associates

Keith Bright has been a prominent figure in the design community for over thirty years. In 1977, he formed his own firm which has grown to include over fifty design and marketing professionals in Los Angeles and New York.

Today, he directs Bright & Associates, a subsidiary of Chiat/Day/Mojo Advertising, in the development of corporate and brand identity, graphic communication, environmental design and packaging. His client list includes Ashton-Tate, Burlington Air Express, Carnation, Holland American Line, Host International, Los Angeles 1984 Olympic Games, National Car Rental, Princess Cruises and Ryder Systems.

"In more recently-designed entries, I could see a certain freeness in design enabled, in many instances, by the computer."

Joel Fuller

Pinkhaus Design Corporation

In 1984, Joel Fuller left behind the fast pace of a New York advertising agency for the calmer and sunnier climate of Pinkhaus, his own Miami design firm.

Pinkhaus was soon boasting such clients as Sterling, a high-end British Leyland automobile, The Lowe Art Museum, Sensi Sportswear, Spec's, a chain of over forty Florida record stores, Aria-Advanced Eyewear from France, and Royal Viking Cruise Lines.

Widely recognized, Joel has received many awards, including those from *Communication Arts, Graphis International,* The One Show, Art Directors Club of New York, *Print, Photo Design, HOW,* Type Directors Club of New York and the AIGA Book Show.

"I was amazed at the impression that marks on paper left with me."

Julia LaPine

Hornall Anderson Design Works

Julia LaPine opened her own graphics firm with a colleague of hers in 1983. She then went on to complete a Master of Fine Arts degree at the University of Utah and to teach design there as well.

Awards from *Communication Arts*, *Print*, New York and Salt Lake City Art Directors Clubs, *Graphis*, AIGA and many others, along with write-ups in such publications as *HOW*, have given national attention to her abilities.

She is most proud of her work with such clients as the Utah Arts Festival, Ririe/Woodbury Dance Company, Jonathan Bell, St. Marks Hospital, and Stephen R. Covey and Associates.

Having recently left her hometown of Salt Lake City, Julia is now employed at the Seattle-based firm of Hornall Anderson Design Works.

"Seeing so many international entries was refreshing and enlightening"

Rex Peteet

Sibley/Peteet Design

Since 1975, Rex Peteet has worked with several prestigious advertising and design firms before creating his own Dallas-based company, with partner Don Sibley, eight years ago.

His work has appeared frequently in such publications as *Communication Arts* and the *New York Art Directors Show Annual,* as well as in *Print, Graphis* and the *American Institute of Graphic Arts Design Annual.* He is also permanently represented in exhibitions at the Library of Congress and the Museum of Modern Art in Hiroshima.

Active with the Dallas Society of Visual Communications, Rex is also one of the founding members of the Texas chapter of AIGA.

"I think the winning entries foretell a movement toward experimental and unusual imagery. Companies are realizing that smaller, more 'private' looks are appreciated for appropriate products and services."

Valerie Richardson

Richardson or Richardson

Richardson or Richardson is a partnership of Valerie and Forrest Richardson, who not only work together, but manage to be married as well. As a partner, she serves as creative director, writer, and designer and is a member of the AIGA and the Phoenix Society of Communication Arts.

The firm has been featured in several publications, including *Adweek, Print, ID, Design Journal of Korea, HOW, Communication Arts* and *Marketing,* a text book. The firm has received various awards, including recognition from the AIGA, *Communication Arts*, the New York Art Directors Club, The Typographic Industry of America, *Photo Design* magazine, *Print's Regional Design Annual* and the Arizona Prisma Awards.

"The best logos were designed with an image of the product in mind. Overly cute or clever didn't cut it in most instances."

Pat Taylor

Pat Taylor, Inc.

A member of the graphic design community since 1953, Pat Taylor has been directing his own firm since 1969.

He has received awards from the Chicago, Iowa, Omaha, Wisconsin, and Washington Metropolitan Art Directors Clubs. The Typographers International Association, Society of Publication Designers, National Composition Association, The Ozzie Awards, AIGA 50 and Washington Trademark Design have also recognized his talents. His work has been published in Japan, Mexico, and the United States. In 1984, the U.S. Postal Service issued a 20–cent envelope recognizing small business, which Pat designed.

CALL FOR

This summer a first-of-its-kind event will take place. An international competition of the eighties' best logos! A half-dozen of our industry's leading designers will be judging marks designed over the past ten years.

Invited to participate are members of the design communities from the U.S. and a score of other countries. Winning entries will be publicly displayed and published. Submit your best work today!

TRADE MARKS OF THE *1980S*

ENTRIES

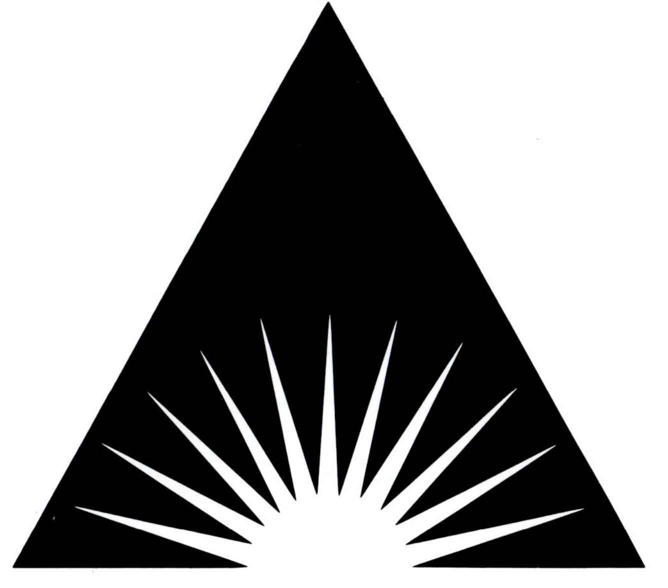

Category:
Logo
Country:
Canada
Year Produced:
1984
Art Director:
Gus Tsetsekas
Designer:
Gus Tsetsekas
Design Firm:
Signals Design Group, Inc.
Client:
Atlanta Gold Corporation

Category:
Logo
Country:
USA
Year Produced:
1985
Art Director:
Keith Bright
Designer:
Peter Sargent and Raymond Wood
Design Firm:
Bright & Associates
Client:
Ashton-Tate, Inc.

The American Institute of Architects, *Cleveland Chapter* 410 The Arcade, Cleveland Ohio 44114, Phone 216 771-1240

Category:
Stationery
Country:

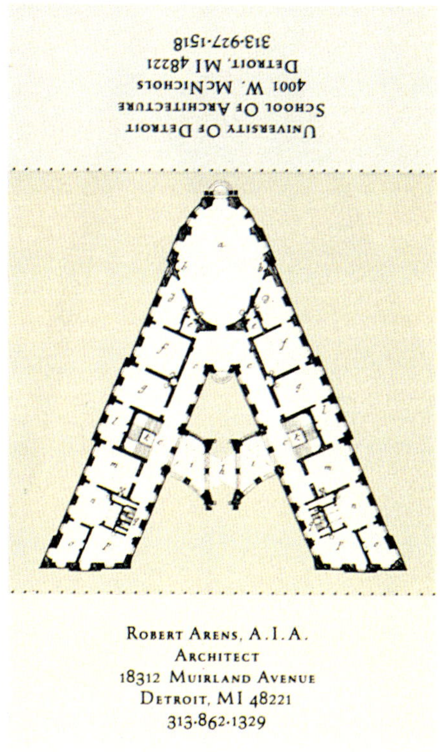

Category:
Logo Application
Country:
USA
Year Produced:
1989
Art Director:
Kim Dent-Levy and Donna McGuire
Designer:
Donna McGuire
Design Firm:
Primadonna
Client:
Robert Arens, *Architect*

Category:
Logo
Country:
Germany
Year Produced:
1984
Art Director:
Heinz Kippnick
Designer:
Heinz Kippnick
Design Firm:
Gebrauchsgrafiker VBK
Client:
Stadt-Archiv Schwerin

Category:
Logo
Country:
USA
Year Produced:
1986
Art Director:
Pat Taylor
Designer:
Pat Taylor
Design Firm:
Pat Taylor, Inc.
Client:
Albert Tape, Inc.

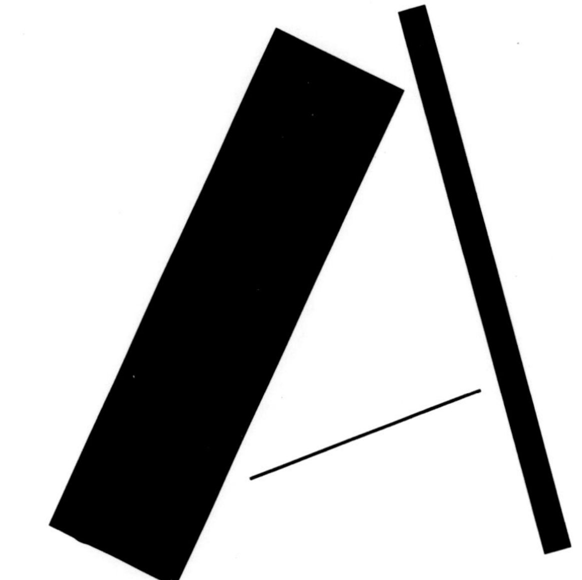

Category:
Logo
Country:
Sweden
Year Produced:
1985
Art Director:
Kari Palmqvist
Designer:
Kari Palmqvist
Design Firm:
Studio Bubblan
Client:
Archigraphic

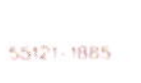

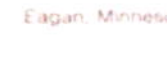

Category:
Stationery
Country:
USA
Year Produced:
1988
Art Director:
Kevin Whaley
Designer:
Kevin Whaley
Design Firm:
Grand Pre' & Whaley, Ltd.
Client:

Category:
Logo
Country:
USA
Year Produced:
1988
Art Director:
Supon Phornirunlit
Designer:
Supon Phornirunlit
Design Firm:
Supon Design Group, Inc.
Client:
Steven T. Bunn, D.D.S.

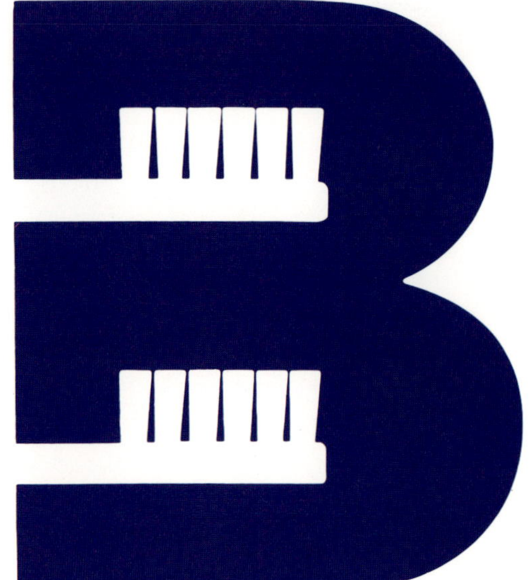

Category:
Logo
Country:
Canada
Year Produced:
1989
Art Director:
Christian Labarthe
Designer:
Christian Labarthe
Design Firm:
Wawa Design
Client:
Brad Mann Communications
Consulting, Inc.

BT

BLANCHET THIBAULT

BT

BLANCHET THIBAULT

Société de courtage en information

37, boulevard St-Joseph, Hull (Québec) J8Y 3V8

téléphone 819·595 2177

Category:
Stationery
Country:
Canada
Year Produced:
1989
Art Director:
Mark Timmings
Designer:
Mario Godbout
Design Firm:
Turquoise Design, Inc.

Category:
Logo Application
Country:
Canada
Year Produced:
1989
Art Director:
John Hardaker
Designer:
Kirsti Ronback
Design Firm:
Rushton Green & Grossutti, Inc.
Client:
Radio Daze

Category:
Logo
Country:
USA
Year Produced:
1987
Art Director:
Rex Peteet and Tom White
Designer:
Rex Peteet
Design Firm:
Sibley/Peteet Design
Client:
Saunders, Lubinski & White

Category:
Logo
Country:
Sweden
Year Produced:
1988
Art Director:
Kari Palmqvist
Designer:
Kari Palmqvist
Design Firm:
Studio Bubblan
Client:
Bjorsells Persondatorer AB

Category:
Logo
Country:
Hong Kong
Year Produced:
1989
Art Director:
Kan Tai-keung
Designer:
Kan Tai-keung and Freeman Lau Siu-hong
Design Firm:
Kan Tai-keung Design & Associates, Ltd.
Client:
East East Wonton Noodle
Restaurant, Ltd.

Category:
Logo Application
Country:
Hong Kong
Year Produced:
1989
Art Director:
Kan Tai-keung
Designer:
Kan Tai-keung and Freeman Lau Siu-hong
Design Firm:
Kan Tai-keung Design & Associates, Ltd.
Client:
East East Wonton Noodle
Restaurant, Ltd.

Category:
Identity Campaign
Country:
Hong Kong
Year Produced:
1989
Art Director:
Kan Tai-keung
Designer:
Kan Tai-keung and Freeman Lau Siu-hong
Design Firm:
Kan Tai-keung Design & Associates, Ltd.
Client:
East East Wonton Noodle
Restaurant, Ltd.

Category:
Logo
Country:
USA
Year Produced:
1986
Art Director:
Nancy Sisk
Designer:
Dick Sisk
Design Firm:
Noah's Art
Client:
Galley Productions, Ltd.

Category:
Logo
Country:
Spain
Year Produced:
1985
Art Director:
Onesim Colavidas
Designer:
Onesim Colavidas
Design Firm:
Design Onesim Colavidas, S.A.
Client:
Grup 3, S.A.

Category:
Logo
Country:
USA
Year Produced:
1986
Art Director:
Woody Pirtle
Designer:
Woody Pirtle
Design Firm:
Pentagram
Client:
Hilton Typographers

Category:
Logo
Country:
USA
Year Produced:
1987
Art Director:
Pat Taylor
Designer:
Pat Taylor
Design Firm:
Pat Taylor, Inc.
Client:
Hastings Development Corporation

Category:
Logo
Country:
USA
Year Produced:
1986
Art Director:
Diane Fannon, Rex Peteet and Don Sibley
Designer:
Walter Horton
Design Firm:
Sibley/Peteet Design
Client:
Tracy-Locke/Haggar Apparel

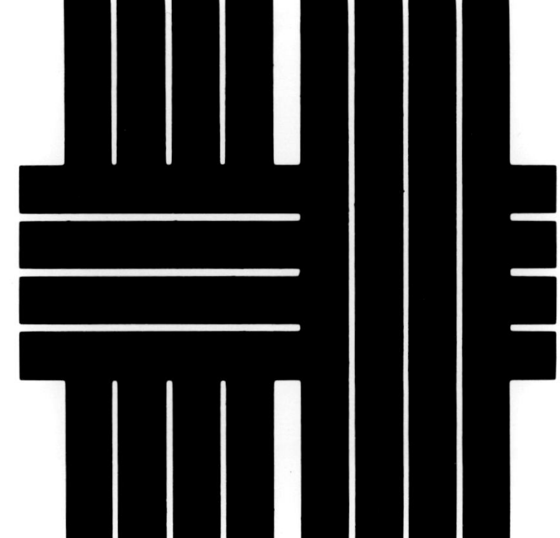

Category:
Logo
Country:
USA
Year Produced:
1987
Art Director:
Jack Hermsen
Designer:
Jack Hermsen
Design Firm:
Hermsen Design Associates, Inc.
Client:
Hermsen Design Associates, Inc.

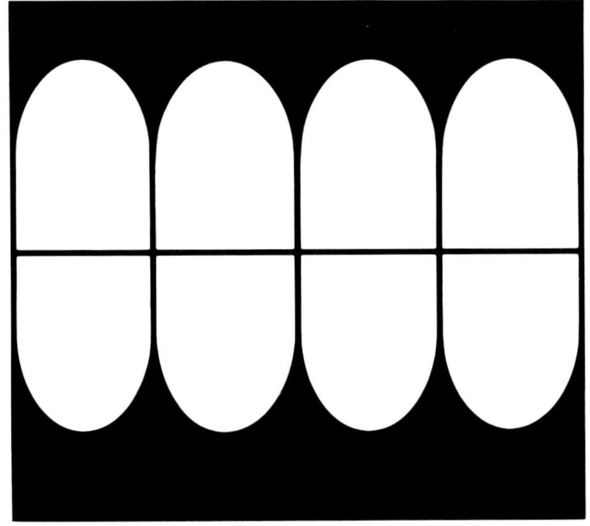

Category:
Logo
Country:
USA
Year Produced:
1987
Art Director:
Rex Peteet
Designer:
Rex Peteet
Design Firm:
Sibley/Peteet Design
Client:
Howard Hudspeth, D.D.S.

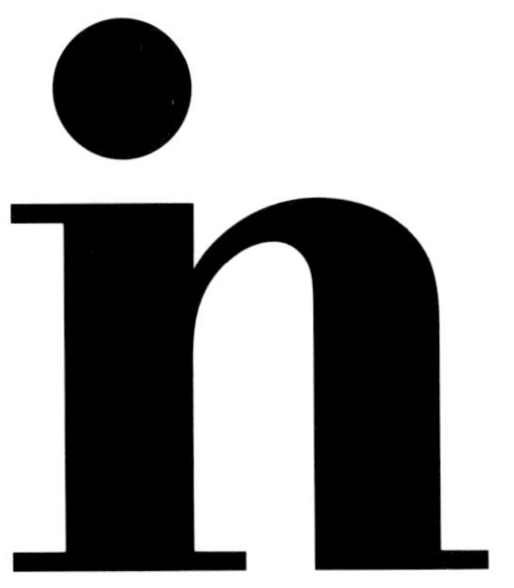

Category:
Logo
Country:
USA
Year Produced:
1988
Art Director:
Barry Deutsch
Designer:
Barry Deutsch
Design Firm:
SBG Partners
Client:
Interactive Network, Inc.

Category:
Logo
Country:
USA
Year Produced:
1981
Art Director:
Jim Lienhart
Designer:
Jim Lienhart
Design Firm:
Murrie Lienhart & Associates
Client:
International Typetronics

Category:
Logo
Country:
USA
Year Produced:
1985
Art Director:
Samuel Kuo
Designer:
Samuel Kuo
Design Firm:
Samuel Kuo Design
Client:
K-Mart Department Stores

Category:
Logo
Country:
USA
Year Produced:
1988
Art Director:
Nicolas Sidjakov
Designer:
Mark Bergman
Design Firm:
SBG Partners
Client:
California State Lottery

Category:
Logo
Country:
Canada
Year Produced:
1983
Art Director:
Stuart Ash
Designer:
Stuart Ash, Richard Kerr and Jenny Leibundgut
Design Firm:
Gottschalk+Ash International
Client:
Ontario Lottery Corporation

Category:
Logo Application
Country:
Netherlands
Year Produced:
1988
Art Director:
Andre Toet
Designer:
Andre Toet
Design Firm:
Samenwerkende Ontwerpers
Client:
Mors Ceiling Construction Company

Category:
Packaging
Country:
USA
Year Produced:
1988
Art Director:
Primo Angeli
Designer:
Ray Honda and Vicki Cero
Design Firm:
Primo Angeli, Inc.
Client:
Shaklee Corporation

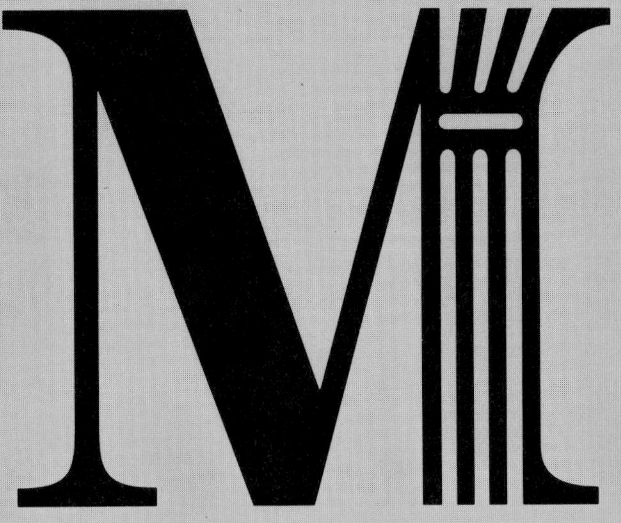

Category:
Logo
Country:
USA
Year Produced:
1988
Art Director:
Jack Anderson
Designer:
Jack Anderson, Cliff Chung and Brian O'Neill
Design Firm:
Hornall Anderson Design Works
Client:
Mithun Partners

Category:
Logo
Country:
Mexico
Year Produced:
1986
Art Director:
Felix Beltran
Designer:
Felix Beltran
Design Firm:
Felix Beltran & Associates
Client:
Nunez, S.A.

Category:
Logo
Country:
USA
Year Produced:
1987
Art Director:
James M. Keeler
Designer:
James M. Keeler
Design Firm:
Gunn Associates
Client:
Nashoba Systems, Inc.

Category:
Logo
Country:
USA
Year Produced:
1987
Art Director:
Keith Bright
Designer:
Alan Rellaford
Design Firm:
Bright & Associates
Client:
National Car Rental System, Inc.

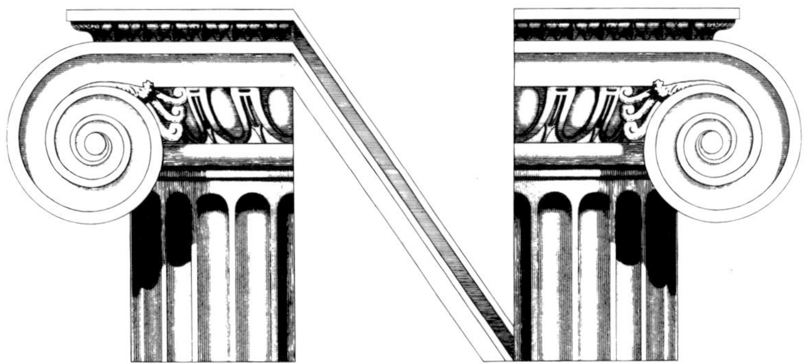

Category:
Logo
Country:
Canada
Year Produced:
1983
Art Director:
Neville Smith
Designer:
Neville Smith
Design Firm:
Neville Smith Graphic Design
Client:
Novara Holdings, Inc.

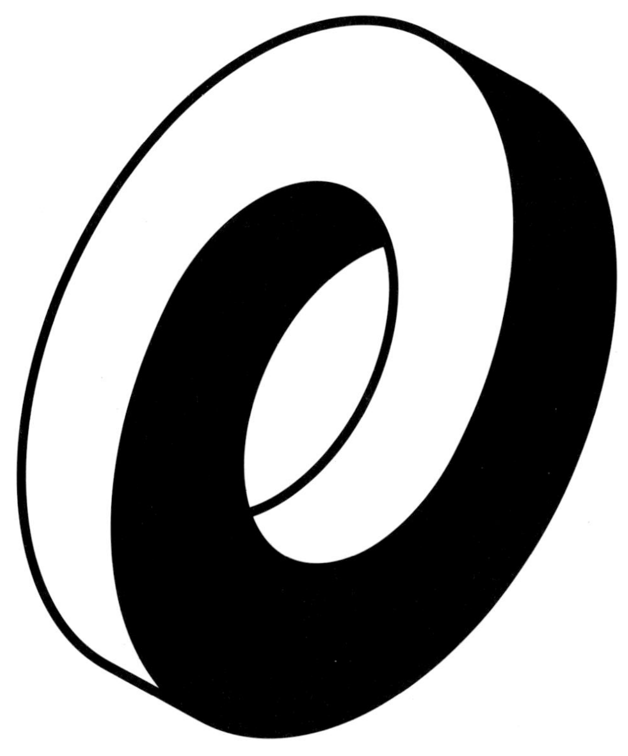

Category:
Logo
Country:
Austria
Year Produced:
1980
Art Director:
Mag. Friedrich Eisenmenger
Designer:
Mag. Friedrich Eisenmenger
Design Firm:
Friedrich Eisenmenger Graphic Design
Client:
Kirchner+Company Internationale
Spedition AG

Category:
Logo
Country:
USA
Year Produced:
1985
Art Director:
John Coy
Designer:
Sean Alatorre and Tom Bouman
Design Firm:
COY
Client:
The Riordan Foundation

Category:
Logo
Country:
USA
Year Produced:
1987
Art Director:
Darin Klundt
Designer:
Darin Klundt
Design Firm:
Klundt & Hosmer Design Associates
Client:
Rowlett Construction, Inc.

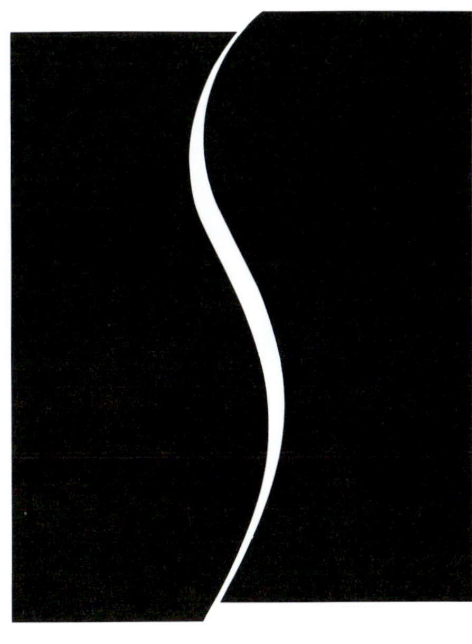

Category:
Logo
Country:
USA
Year Produced:
1988
Art Director:
Gill Fishman
Designer:
Louise Sandhaus
Design Firm:
Gill Fishman Associates
Client:
Saber Software

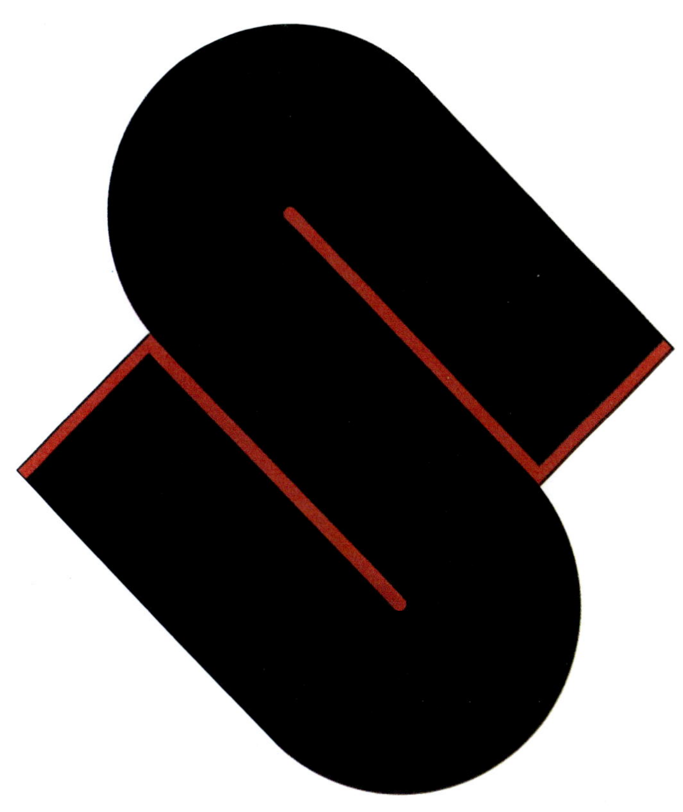

Category:
Logo
Country:
Germany
Year Produced:
1983
Art Director:
Achim Kiel AGD
Designer:
Achim Kiel AGD
Design Firm:
Pencil Corporate Art
Client:
Si-Technik GmbH

Category:
Logo
Country:
USA
Year Produced:
1987
Art Director:
John Evans
Designer:
John Evans
Design Firm:
Sibley/Peteet Design
Client:
Patricia Silverman, *Creative Consultant*

Category:
Logo
Country:
USA
Year Produced:
1980
Art Director:
Robert Miles Runyan
Designer:
Robert Miles Runyan
Design Firm:
Robert Miiles Runyan & Associates
Client:
Unisource Corporation

Category:
Stationery
Country:
Australia
Year Produced:
1988
Art Director:
Annette Harcus
Designer:
Annette Harcus
Design Firm:
Annette Harcus Design
Client:
Tuileries Restaurant
Illustrator:
Melinda Dudley

Category:
Logo
Country:
Japan
Year Produced:
1980
Art Director:
Shigeo Katsuoka
Designer:
Shigeo Katsuoka
Design Firm:
Shigeo Katsuoka Design Studio
Client:
Urbanet Corporation

Category:
Logo
Country:
Japan
Year Produced:
1989
Art Director:
Douglas Doolittle
Designer:
Douglas Doolittle
Design Firm:
Douglas Design Office
Client:
Vasara

Category:
Logo
Country:
USA
Year Produced:
1988
Art Director:
Supon Phornirunlit
Designer:
Supon Phornirunlit
Design Firm:
Supon Design Group, Inc.
Client:
Walsh Wallpaper

Category:
Logo
Country:
USA
Year Produced:
1988
Art Director:
D.C. Stipp
Designer:
D.C. Stipp
Design Firm:
Richards, Brock, Miller, Mitchell & Associates
Client:
Willis Painting Contractors

Category:
Stationery
Country:
USA
Year Produced:
1989
Art Director:

Category:
Logo
Country:
USA
Year Produced:
1989
Art Director:
Claude Salzberger and Don Kline
Designer:
Joe Finocchiaro and Don Kline
Design Firm:
Landor Associates
Client:
Northwest Airlines, Inc.

Category:
Logo
Country:
Mexico
Year Produced:
1983
Art Director:
Felix Beltran
Designer:
Felix Beltran
Design Firm:
Felix Beltran & Associates
Client:
Xpos, S.A.

Category:
Logo
Country:
USA
Year Produced:
1989
Art Director:
Hien Nguyen
Designer:
Hien Nguyen and Stephanie Hooton
Design Firm:
Pictogram Studio
Client:
Ecco Cafe

Category:
Logo
Country:
USA
Year Produced:
1985
Art Director:
Jay Vigon and Rick Seireeni
Designer:
Jay Vigon
Design Firm:
Vigon/Seireeni
Client:
Leon Max

Category:
Logo
Country:
USA
Year Produced:
1989
Art Director:
Robert Froedge
Illustrator:
Robert Froedge
Design Firm:
Image Design, Inc.
Client:
Western Civilians

Category:
Logo
Country:
USA
Year Produced:
1989
Art Director:
Nicolas Sidjakov
Designer:
Amy Knapp
Design Firm:
SBG Partners
Client:
EurekaBank

Category:
Logo
Country:
USA
Year Produced:
1989
Art Director:
Nicolas Sidjakov
Designer:
Thomas Bond
Design Firm:
SBG Partners
Client:
Summit Sales

Category:
Logo
Country:
USA
Year Produced:
1989
Art Director:
Stephen Miller
Designer:
Stephen Miller
Design Firm:
Richards, Brock, Miller, Mitchell & Associates
Client:
Mobility Foundation

Category:
Logo
Country:
USA
Year Produced:
1988
Art Director:
Courtney Reeser
Designer:
Tom McNulty and Ben Wheeler
Design Firm:
SBG Partners
Client:
ADVO

Category:
Logo
Country:
USA
Year Produced:
1989
Art Director:
Dennis Walston
Designer:
Jim Gray
Design Firm:
The Kamber Group
Client:
Independent Artists Committee For Democratic Change in Eastern Europe

Category:
Logo
Country:
England
Year Produced:
1988
Art Director:
Tor Pettersen
Designer:
Tor Pettersen, Colleen Crim and Claire Barnett
Design Firm:
Tor Pettersen & Partners
Client:
Environmental Management, Ltd.

Category:
Logo
Country:
USA
Year Produced:
1988
Art Director:
John Coy
Designer:
John Coy
Design Firm:
COY
Client:
UCLA College of Fine Arts

Category:
Logo
Country:
USA
Year Produced:
1988
Art Director:
Martin Carrichner
Designer:
Martin Carrichner
Design Firm:
Martin Carrichner's Design Sense
Client:
Sidekicks Ensemble

Category:
Logo
Country:
USA
Year Produced:
1989
Art Director:
Barry A. Merten
Designer:
Lani Dolifka
Design Firm:
Merten Design Group
Client:
Colorado Council on the Arts
and Humanities

THE DANDY CANDY MAN
Purveyor of Condommints

POST OFFICE BOX 2151
LOS GATOS, CA 95031
PHONE · 408.378.5600
TELEFAX · 408.354.1450

KELLY O'CONNOR
HEAD CANDY MAN

THE DANDY CANDY MAN
Purveyor of Condommints

POST OFFICE BOX 2151
LOS GATOS, CA 95031
PHONE · 408.378.5600
TELEFAX · 408.354.1450

Category:
Logo
Country:
Australia
Year Produced:
1989
Art Director:
Barrie Tucker
Designer:
Barrie Tucker
Design Firm:
Barrie Tucker Design Pty, Ltd.
Client:
Negociants International
Artist:
Paul Dowell

Category:
Logo
Country:
Canada
Year Produced:
1989
Art Director:
Neville Smith
Designer:
Neville Smith
Design Firm:
Neville Smith Graphic Design
Client:
The Cadillac Fairview Corporation/
Victoria Eaton Centre

Category:
Logo
Country:
USA
Year Produced:
1985
Art Director:
Ken Shafer
Designer:
Ken Shafer
Design Firm:
Richards, Brock, Miller, Mitchell & Associates

Category:
Logo
Country:
Hong Kong
Year Produced:
1987
Art Director:
Alan Chan
Designer:
Alan Chan and Phillip Leung
Design Firm:
Alan Chan Design Company
Client:
Toyo Hotel

Category:
Logo
Country:
Hong Kong
Year Produced:
1986
Art Director:
Kan Tai-keung
Designer:
Kan Tai-Keung and Eddy Yu Chi-kong
Design Firm:
Kan Tai-Keung Design & Associates, Ltd.
Client:
Lutex Company, Ltd.

Category:
Logo
Country:
USA
Year Produced:
1984
Art Director:
Gerald Gallo
Designer:
Gerald Gallo
Design Firm:
Graphics By Gallo
Client:
Virginia Graphics, Inc.

Category:
Logo Application
Country:
USA
Year Produced:
1987
Art Director:
Jack Anderson and Cheri Huber
Designer:
Jack Anderson, Julie Tanagi-Lock, Mary Hermes and Cheri Huber
Design Firm:
Hornall Anderson Design Works
Client:
Tradewell

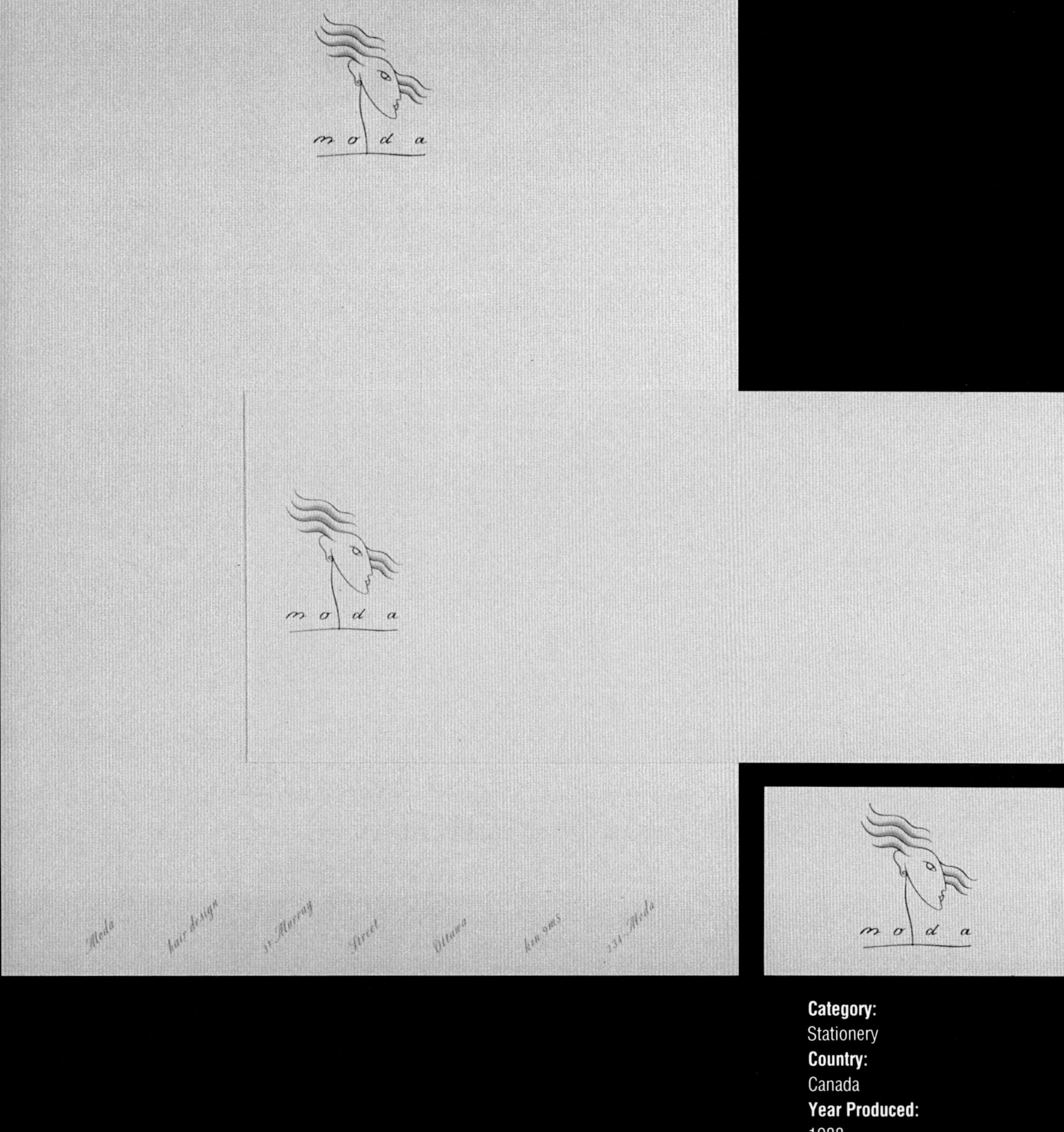

Category:
Stationery
Country:
Canada
Year Produced:
1988
Art Director:
Neville Smith
Designer:
Neville Smith
Design Firm:
Neville Smith Graphic Design
Client:

Category:
Logo
Country:
Canada
Year Produced:
1988
Art Director:
Neville Smith
Designer:
Neville Smith
Design Firm:
Neville Smith Graphic Design
Client:
Moda Hair Design

Category:
Logo
Country:
USA
Year Produced:
1988
Art Director:
Nicolas Sidjakov and Barbara Vick
Designer:
Jackie Foshaug
Design Firm:
SBG Partners
Client:
Samaritan Foundation
Illustrator:
Rebecca Archey

SAMARITAN

Category:
Logo
Country:
USA
Year Produced:
1989
Art Director:
Jeanne Greco
Designer:
Jeanne Greco
Design Firm:
Caffe Greco Design
Client:
The Fragrance Shoppe

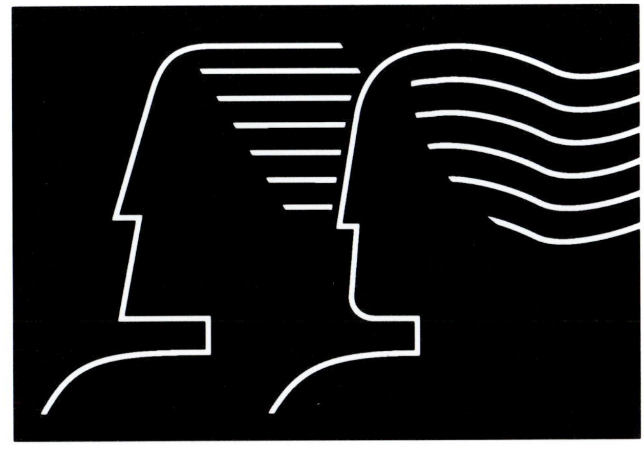

Category:
Logo
Country:
USA
Year Produced:
1987
Art Director:
Craig Thomas
Designer:
Craig Thomas
Design Firm:
Craig Thomas Graphic Design
Client:
Dennis Capoz, Headquarters for Hair

Category:
Logo
Country:
Spain
Year Produced:
1989
Art Director:
Sonsoles Llorens
Designer:
Sonsoles Llorens
Design Firm:
Sonsoles Llorens
Client:
Ville de Marseille

BIENNALE DES JEUNES
CRÉATEURS D'EUROPE
DE LA MÉDITERRANÉE

Category:
Logo
Country:
USA
Year Produced:
1982
Art Director:
Don Sibley
Designer:
Don Sibley
Design Firm:
Sibley/Peteet Design
Client:
Jan Harmon, *Children's Art Instructor*

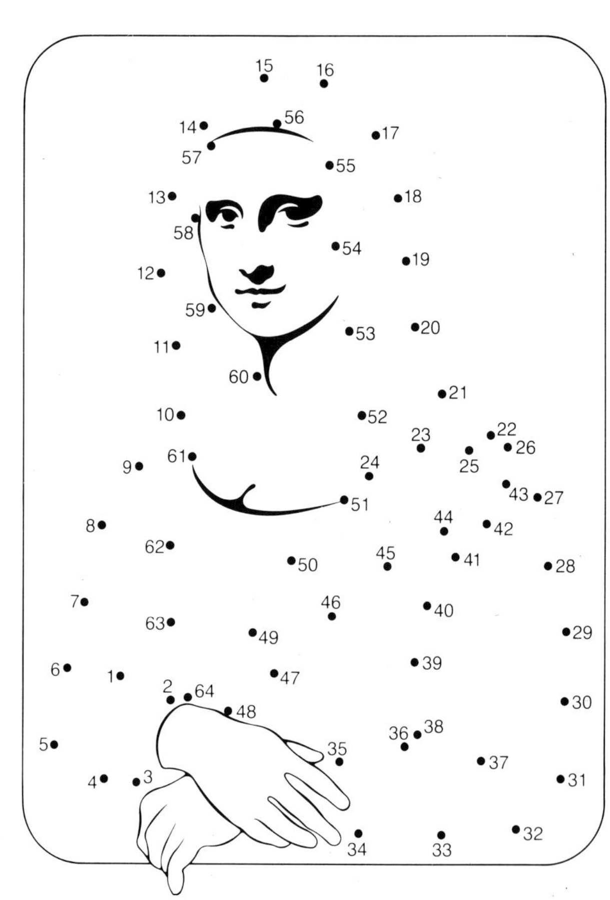

Ville de Marseille
Services des Affaires Culturelles
14 Rue Beauvau 13001 Marseille
Tel: 91 541000 Fax: 91 552464

Marseille 1990

Biennale des Jeunes
Créateurs d'Europe
de la Méditerranée

Marseille 1990

Biennale des Jeunes
Créateurs d'Europe
de la Méditerranée

Ville de Marseille
Services des Affaires Culturelles
14 Rue Beauvau 13001 Marseille
Tel 91 541000 Fax 91 552464

Marseille 1990

Biennale des Jeunes
Créateurs d'Europe
de la Méditerranée

Ville de Marseille
Services des Affaires Culturelles
14 Rue Beauvau 13001 Marseille
Tel 91 541000 Fax 91 552464

Category:

Category:
Logo
Country:
USSR
Year Produced:
1980
Art Director:
Marat Bejajev
Designer:
Marat Bejajev
Design Firm:
Sobyetvienost Avtora
Client:
Marat Bejajev

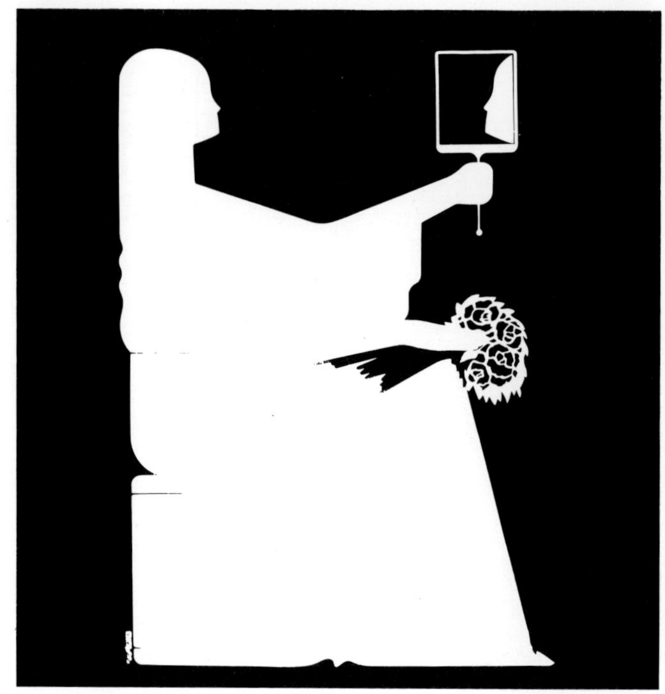

Category:
Logo
Country:
USA
Year Produced:
1987
Art Director:
Jay Vigon and Rick Seireeni
Designer:
Jay Vigon
Design Firm:
Vigon/Seireeni
Client:
Flaming Colossus

Category:
Logo
Country:
USA
Year Produced:
1987
Art Director:
Bill Stitzel, Don Sibley and Rex Peteet
Designer:
Rex Peteet
Design Firm:
Sibley/Peteet Design
Client:
Mary Kay Cosmetics

Category:
Logo Application
Country:
USA
Year Produced:
1989
Art Director:
Regina Rubino
Designer:
Robert Louey
Design Firm:
Louey/Rubino Design Group
Client:
Fleurs du Jour
Illustrator:
Robert Louey

Category:
Packaging
Country:
USA
Year Produced:
1988
Art Director:
Keith Bright
Designer:
Raymond Wood
Design Firm:
Bright & Associates
Client:
Ethel M Chocolate, Inc.

Category:
Logo
Country:
USA
Year Produced:
1988
Art Director:
Keith Bright
Designer:
Raymond Wood
Design Firm:
Bright & Associates
Client:
TreePeople

Category:
Logo
Country:
USA
Year Produced:
1989
Art Director:
Jack Anderson
Designer:
Jack Anderson, Mary Hermes and David Bates
Design Firm:
Hornall Anderson Design Works
Client:
The Callison Partnership

Category:
Stationery
Country:
Australia
Year Produced:
1989
Art Director:
Annette Harcus
Designer:
Stephanie Martin and Annette Harcus
Design Firm:
Annette Harcus Design
Client:
Kalacraft Fiji, Ltd.
Illustrator:
Melinda Dudley

Category:
Logo
Country:
USA
Year Produced:
1984
Art Director:
Keith Bright
Designer:
Peter Sargent
Design Firm:
Bright & Associates
Client:
800 Flowers, Inc.

Category:
Logo
Country:
Australia
Year Produced:
1988
Art Director:
Annette Harcus
Designer:
Annette Harcus
Design Firm:
Annette Harcus Design
Client:
Windsor Castle Bar & Restaurant

WINDSOR CASTLE HOTEL
CORNER OF WINDSOR AND ELIZABETH STREETS · PADDINGTON
NSW 2021 · AUSTRALIA · TELEPHONE (02)·32 2757

Category:
Logo
Country:
Australia
Year Produced:
1989
Art Director:
Annette Harcus
Designer:
Annette Harcus
Design Firm:
Annette Harcus Design
Client:
The Northrock Group

Category:
Logo
Country:
USA
Year Produced:
1980
Art Director:
Simms Taback
Designer:
Michael Doret
Design Firm:
Michael Doret, Inc.
Client:
Graphic Artists Guild

Category:
Stationery
Country:

Category:
Stationery
Country:

Category:
Packaging
Country:
USA
Year Produced:
1984
Art Director:
Primo Angeli
Designer:
Primo Angeli
Design Firm:
Primo Angeli, Inc.
Client:
P.G. Molinari & Sons
Illustrator:
Mark Jones

Category:
Packaging
Country:
USA
Year Produced:
1987
Art Director:
Nicolas Sidjakov and Jerry Berman
Designer:
Mark Bergman
Design Firm:
SBG Partners
Client:
Kraft Foods
Illustrator:
Dave Stevenson

Category:
Packaging
Country:
USA
Year Produced:
1988
Art Director:
John Sayles
Designer:
John Sayles
Design Firm:
Sayles Graphic Design, Inc.
Client:
Drake University

Category:
Logo
Country:
USA
Year Produced:
1982
Art Director:
Michael Doret
Designer:
Michael Doret
Design Firm:
Michael Doret, Inc.
Client:
Margarethe Hubauer GmbH

Category:
Logo
Country:
Australia
Year Produced:
1989
Art Director:
Annette Harcus
Designer:
Annette Harcus
Design Firm:
Annette Harcus Design
Client:
Chocolate Works

Category:
Stationery
Country:
USA
Year Produced:
1989
Art Director:
Mike Zender
Designer:
Diane Cartheuser and Priscilla A.W. Fisher
Design Firm:
Zender+Associates, Inc.
Client:
Adams Landing Ltd. Partnership

Category:
Stationery
Country:
USA
Year Produced:
1989
Art Director:
Okey Nestor
Designer:
Okey Nestor
Design Firm:
Nesnadny & Schwartz
Client:
International Asset Management

Category:
Packaging
Country:
USA
Year Produced:
1985
Art Director:
Nicolas Sidjakov and Jerry Berman
Designer:
James Nevins
Design Firm:
SBG Partners
Client:
Welch Foods, Inc.
Illustrator:
Gregg Keeling

Category:
Packaging
Country:
USA
Year Produced:
1987
Art Director:
Nicolas Sidjakov and Jerry Berman
Designer:
Dave Curtis
Design Firm:
SBG Partners
Client:
Universal Foods

SAYLES
GRAPHIC
DESIGN

SAYLES
GRAPHIC
DESIGN

SAYLES
GRAPHIC
DESIGN
JOHN SAYLES
308 Eighth Street Des Moines Iowa 50309 515-243-2922 Fax 243-0212

Category:

Category:
Logo
Country:
USA
Year Produced:
1985
Art Director:
Jay Vigon and Rick Seireeni
Designer:
Jay Vigon
Design Firm:
Vigon/Seireeni
Client:
B.J. Designs

Category:
Logo
Country:
Canada
Year Produced:
1989
Art Director:
Amanda Finn
Designer:
Amanda Finn
Design Firm:
Lawrence Finn & Associates, Ltd.
Client:
Mathesis, Inc./Fiscal Knowledge

Category:
Stationery
Country:
USA
Year Produced:
1989
Art Director:
Rick Tharp
Designer:
Rick Tharp and Kim Tomlinson
Design Firm:
Tharp Did It

Category:
Logo Application
Country:
USA
Year Produced:
1980
Art Director:
Tom Curry
Designer:
Tom Curry
Design Firm:
Prickly Pear Studio
Client:
Tom Curry

Category:
Packaging
Country:
USA
Year Produced:
1989
Art Director:
Keith Bright
Designer:
Raymond Wood and Barbara Eadie
Design Firm:
Bright & Associates
Client:
Los Angeles Brewing Company

Category:
Logo
Country:
USA
Year Produced:
1989
Art Director:
Keith Bright
Designer:
Raymond Wood
Design Firm:
Bright & Associates
Client:
Los Angeles Brewing Company

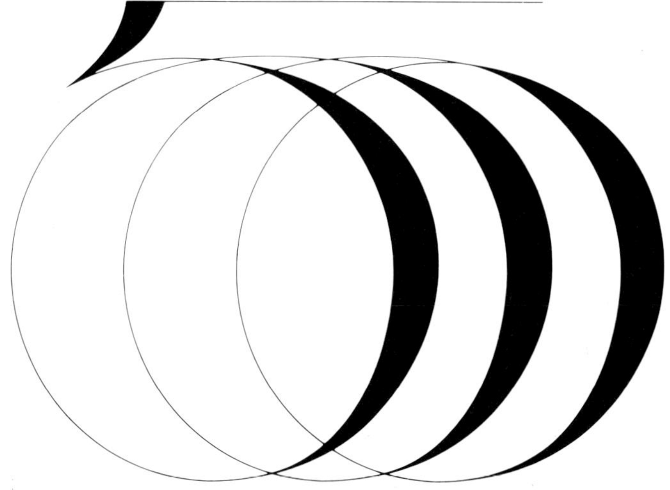

Category:
Logo
Country:
USA
Year Produced:
1984
Art Director:
D.C. Stipp
Designer:
D.C. Stipp
Design Firm:
Richards, Brock, Miller, Mitchell & Associates
Client:
500, Inc.

Category:
Packaging
Country:
USA
Year Produced:
1987
Art Director:
Jack Anderson
Designer:
Jack Anderson and Mary Hermes
Design Firm:
Hornall Anderson Design Works
Client:
Broadmoor Baker

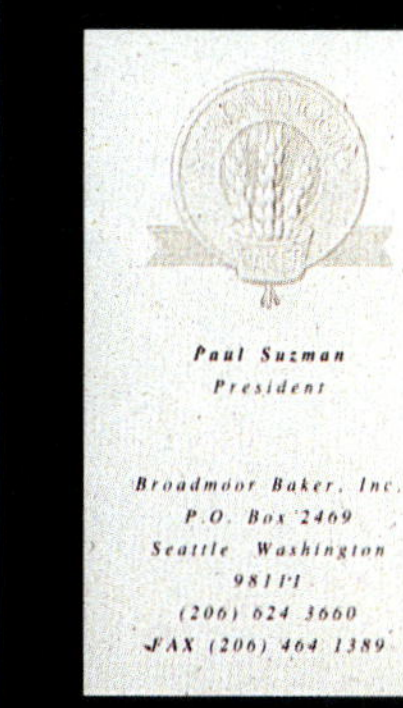

Broadmoor Baker, Inc.
P.O. Box 2469
Seattle Washington 98111
(206) 624 3660 FAX (206) 464 1389

Category:
Stationery
Country:
USA
Year Produced:
1989
Art Director:
Jack Anderson
Designer:

Category:
Packaging
Country:
England
Year Produced:
1989
Art Director:
Chris Lower
Designer:
Andrew Cross
Design Firm:
Design House
Client:
Burton's Biscuits
Illustrator:
Bob Harberfield

Category:
Packaging
Country:
USA
Year Produced:
1986
Art Director:
Hal Riney and Jerry Andelin
Designer:
Primo Angeli
Design Firm:
Primo Angeli, Inc.
Client:
Blitz-Weinhard Company
Illustrator:
Mark Jones

Category:
Logo Application
Country:
USA
Year Produced:
1985
Art Director:
Primo Angeli
Designer:
Primo Angeli
Design Firm:
Primo Angeli, Inc.
Client:
Ultra Lucca Delicatessens
Illustrator:
Mark Jones

Category:
Packaging
Country:
USA
Year Produced:
1980
Art Director:
Primo Angeli
Designer:
Primo Angeli
Design Firm:
Primo Angeli, Inc.
Client:
San Francisco French Bread Company

Category:
Logo Application
Country:
England
Year Produced:
1988
Art Director:
John Larkin
Designer:
John Larkin
Design Firm:
Design House
Client:
The Pheasantry Group

Category:
Logo
Country:
USA
Year Produced:
1987
Art Director:
Steven R. Grigg
Designer:
Steven R. Grigg and Daniel Ruesch
Design Firm:
Tandem Studios
Client:
Whipple & Associates Typography

Category:
Logo
Country:
USA
Year Produced:
1988
Art Director:
Alan Mickelson
Designer:
Alan Mickelson
Design Firm:
Mickelson Design & Associates
Client:
Harmony Business Machines

Category:
Logo
Country:
USA
Year Produced:
1989
Art Director:
Bruce E. Morgan
Designer:
Bruce E. Morgan
Design Firm:
Bruce E. Morgan Graphic Design
Client:
Renee Comet Photography

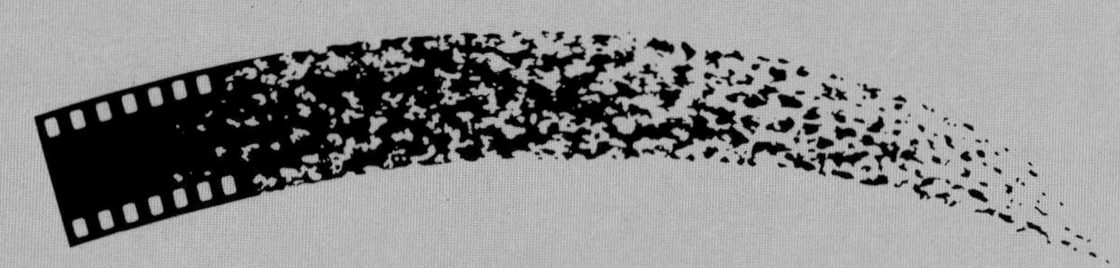

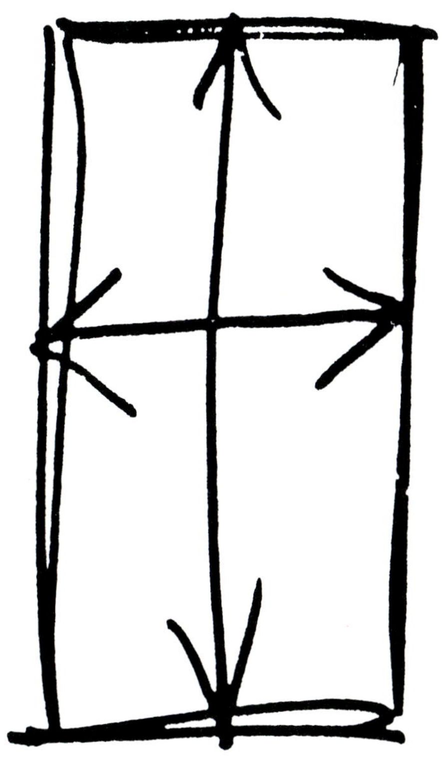

Category:
Logo
Country:
USA
Year Produced:
1982
Art Director:
Pat Taylor
Designer:
Pat Taylor
Design Firm:
Pat Taylor, Inc.
Client:
Art Directors Club of Metropolitan Washington/*Fullbleed* Magazine

Category:
Logo
Country:
USA
Year Produced:
1989
Art Director:
Edward Rebek
Designer:
Joanne Rebek and Ed Rebek
Design Firm:
JOED Design
Client:
Red Tomato, Inc.

Category:
Logo Application
Country:
Japan
Year Produced:
1987
Art Director:
Douglas Doolittle
Designer:
Douglas Doolittle
Design Firm:
Douglas Design Office
Client:
I.D. Corporation

Category:
Packaging
Country:
USA
Year Produced:
1984
Art Director:
Keith Bright
Designer:
Raymond Wood
Design Firm:
Bright & Associates
Client:
Kaepa, Inc.

AR Lithographers
28302/C Industrial Blvd.
Hayward California 94545
Tel: 415.786.2244
Raymond Burnham, Jr.
AR Lithographers
28302/C Industrial Blvd.
Hayward California 94545
Tel. 415.786.2244
28302/C Industrial Blvd.
Hayward California 94545

Category:
Logo Application
Country:
USA
Year Produced:
1986
Art Director:
Mark Anderson
Designer:
Earl Gee
Design Firm:
Mark Anderson Design
Client:
AR Lithographers
Illustrator:
Earl Gee

Category:
Identity Campaign
Country:
USA
Year Produced:
1989
Art Director:
Jack Anderson and Jani Drewfs
Designer:
Jani Drewfs, Jack Anderson and David Bates
Design Firm:
Hornall Anderson Design Works
Client:
Microsoft Universitv

Industry Perspective
The answer to a growing need in a fast-changing industry.
9:00
10:00
11:00
12:00
1:00
2:00
3:00
4:00
MicrosoftUniversity

Microsoft Windows

Labs

Category:
Packaging
Country:
USA
Year Produced:
1987
Art Director:
Kathleen Nelson
Designer:
Glenn Martinez
Design Firm:
Glenn Martinez & Associates
Client:
Caymus Vineyards

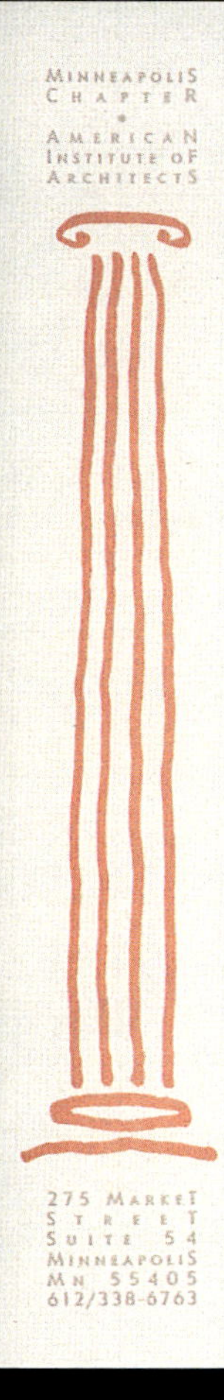

Category:
Stationery
Country:
USA
Year Produced:
1987
Art Director:
Bruce Rubin
Designer:
William Homan
Design Firm:
Rubin Cordaro Design
Client:

Category:
Identity Campaign
Country:
Hong Kong
Year Produced:
1989
Art Director:
Catherine Lam Siu-hung
Designer:
Catherine Lam Siu-hung
Design Firm:
Cat Production
Client:
Card Gallery

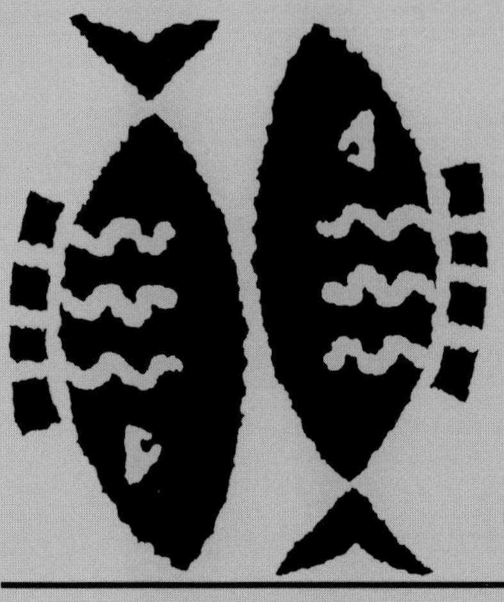

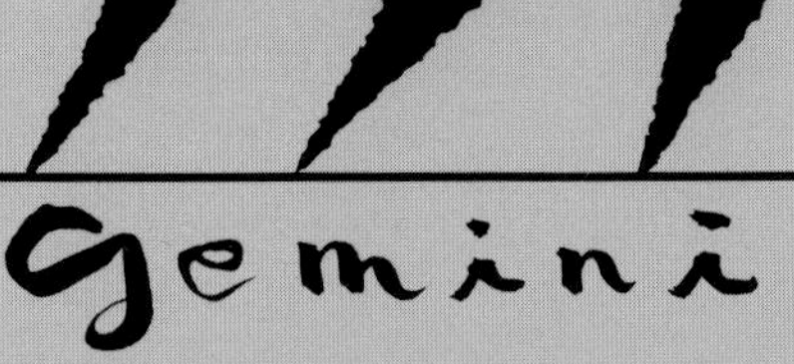

Leo

Virgo

Libra

Scorpio

Sagittarius

Capricorn

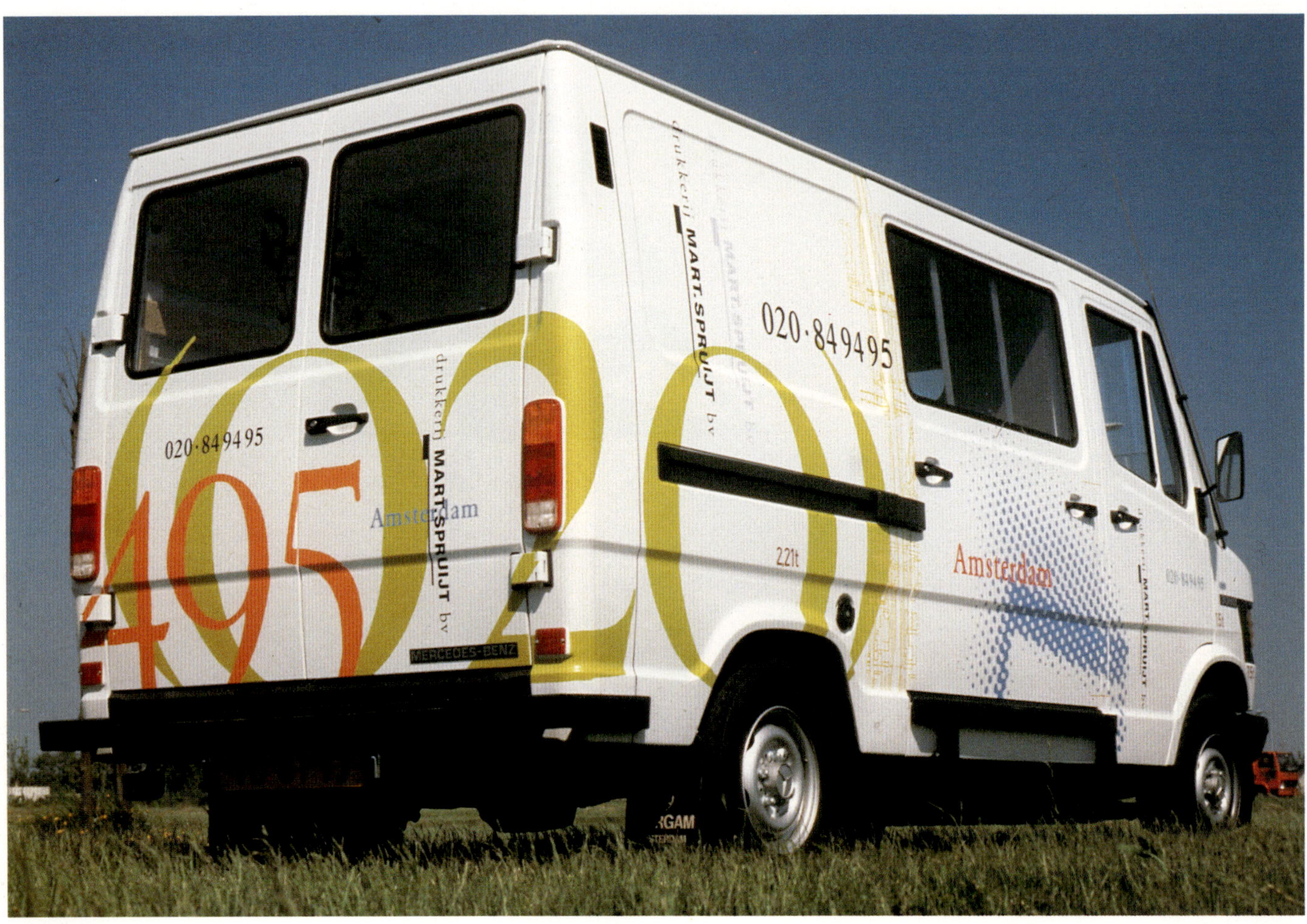

Category:
Logo Application
Country:
Netherlands
Year Produced:
1989
Art Director:
Marianne Vos
Designer:
Marianne Vos
Design Firm:
Samenwerkende Ontwerpers
Client:
Drukkerij Mart. Spruijt bv

Category:
Identity Campaign
Country:
Netherlands
Year Produced:
1989
Art Director:
Marianne Vos
Designer:
Marianne Vos

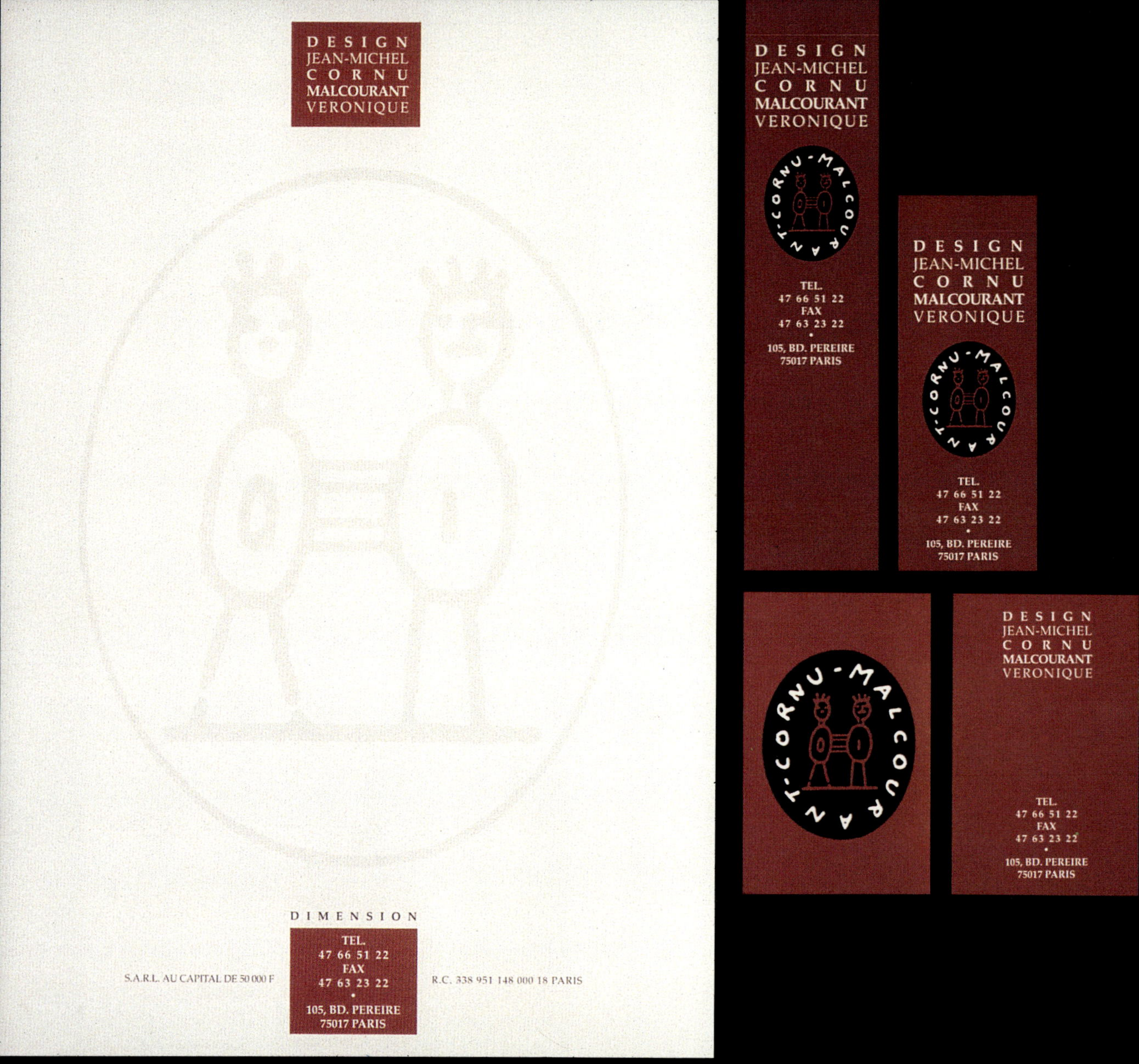

DESIGN
JEAN-MICHEL
CORNU
MALCOURANT
VERONIQUE

DIMENSION

S.A.R.L. AU CAPITAL DE 50 000 F

TEL.
47 66 51 22
FAX
47 63 23 22
•
105, BD. PEREIRE
75017 PARIS

R.C. 338 951 148 000 18 PARIS

Category:
Stationery
Country:
France
Year Produced:
1988
Art Director:
Cornu-Malcourant
Designer:
Cornu-Malcourant
Design Firm:
Cornu-Malcourant
Client:

Category:
Logo
Country:
France
Year Produced:
1988
Art Director:
Cornu-Malcourant
Designer:
Cornu-Malcourant
Design Firm:
Cornu-Malcourant
Client:
Cornu-Malcourant

Category:
Logo Application
Country:
France
Year Produced:
1988
Art Director:
Cornu-Malcourant
Designer:
Cornu-Malcourant
Design Firm:
Cornu-Malcourant
Client:
Cornu-Malcourant

Category:
Logo
Country:
USA
Year Produced:
1989
Art Director:
Antonio Alcala
Designer:
Antonio Alcala
Design Firm:
Studio A
Client:
Time-Life Books/Best Loved Storybooks

Category:
Logo
Country:
USA
Year Produced:
1986
Art Director:
Forrest Richarson
Designer:
Rosemary Connelly
Design Firm:
Richarson or Richardson
Client:
J.W. Tumbles

J.W. TUMBLES

A Children's Gym
5541 Clairemont Mesa Boulevard
San Diego, California 92117
619-279-0988

Jill Ann Schmidt
Director

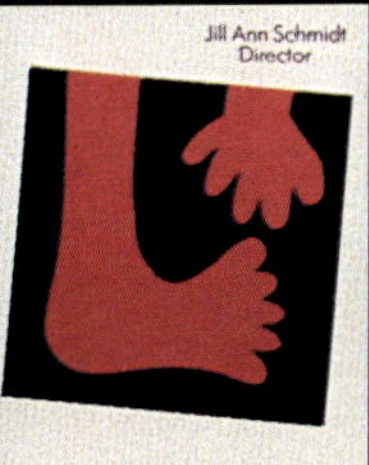

J.W. TUMBLES

A Children's Gym
5541 Clairemont Mesa Boulevard
San Diego, California 92117
619-279-0988

J.W. TUMBLES

A Children's Gym
140 South Solana Hills Drive
Plaza West II Shopping Center
Solana Beach, California 92075
619-481-5576

Category:
Stationery
Country:
USA
Year Produced:
1986
Art Director:
Forrest Richarson
Designer:
Rosemary Connelly
Design Firm:
Richarson or Richardson
Client:

Category:
Stationery
Country:
USA
Year Produced:
1989
Art Director:
Jeffrey L. Dever
Designer:
Jeffrey L. Dever
Design Firm:
Dever Designs, Inc.
Client:
John Snow, Inc./REACH

Category:
Logo
Country:
USA
Year Produced:
1986
Art Director:
Nancy Sisk
Designer:
Dick Sisk
Design Firm:
Noah's Art
Client:
Child Development Center of Northern Virginia

Category:
Logo
Country:
USA
Year Produced:
1984
Art Director:
Kevin Whaley
Designer:
Kevin Whaley
Design Firm:
Grand Pre' and Whaley, Ltd.
Client:
University of Minnesota/ Minnesota Heart Health Program

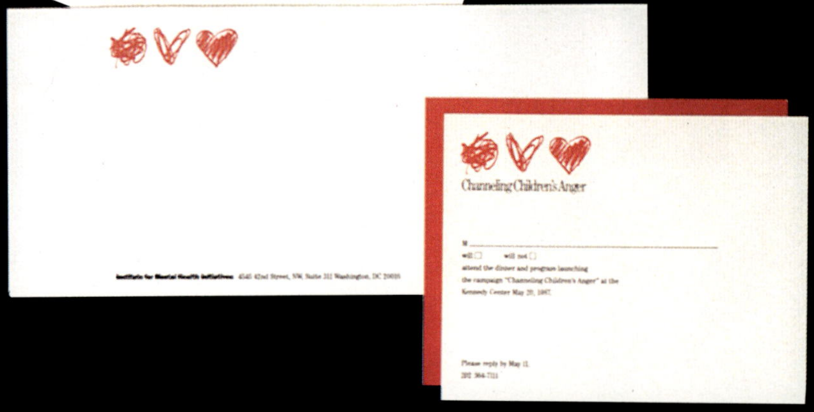

Category:
Identity Campaign
Country:
USA
Year Produced:
1987
Art Director:
Ellen Shapiro
Designer:
Terri Bogaards
Design Firm:
Shapiro Design Associates, Inc.
Client:

Category:
Logo
Country:
USA
Year Produced:
1987
Art Director:
Ellen Shapiro
Designer:
Terri Bogaards
Design Firm:
Shapiro Design Associates, Inc.
Client:
Institute for Mental Health Initiatives

Category:
Logo Application
Country:
USA
Year Produced:
1987
Art Director:
Ellen Shapiro
Designer:
Terri Bogaards
Design Firm:
Shapiro Design Associates, Inc.
Client:
Institute for Mental Health Initiatives

Category:
Stationery
Country:
USA
Year Produced:
1987
Art Director:
Forrest Richardson and Valerie Richardson
Designer:
Forrest Richardson
Design Firm:
Richardson or Richardson
Client:

Category:
Logo
Country:
USA
Year Produced:
1988
Art Director:
John Evans and Jim Bremer
Designer:
John Evans
Design Firm:
Sibley/Peteet Design
Client:
Milton Bradley/Mall Madness Game

Category:
Logo
Country:
Hong Kong
Year Produced:
1988
Art Director:
Alan Chan
Designer:
Alan Chan
Design Firm:
Alan Chan Design Company
Client:
Alan Chan Design Company

Category:
Identity Campaign
Country:
USA
Year Produced:
1986
Art Director:
Forrest Richardson and Valerie Richardson
Designer:
Jim Bolek, Forrest Richardson and

Sunrise
Preschool

Sunrise
My Red
Sunrise Box

Sunrise Preschools
Extra Neat Stuff.

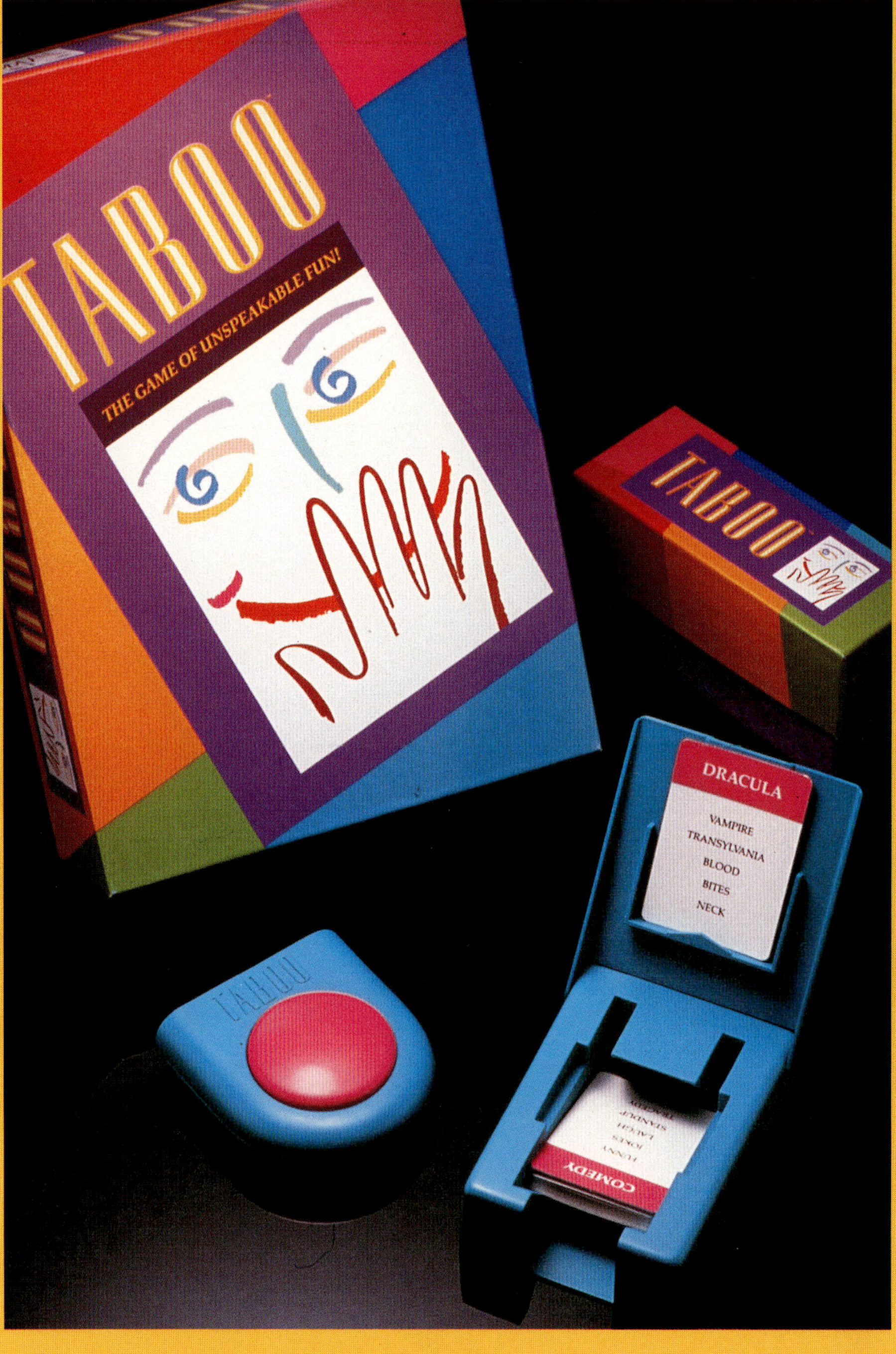

Category:
Packaging
Country:
USA
Year Produced:
1989
Art Director:
Don Sibley and Jim Bremer
Designer:
Don Sibley
Design Firm:
Sibley/Peteet Design
Client:
Milton Bradley

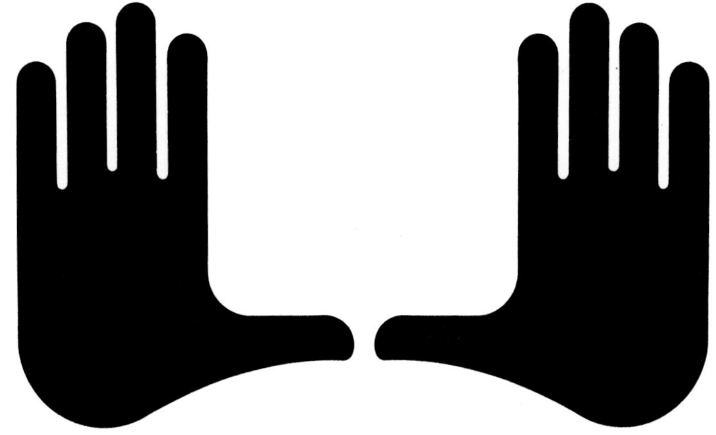

Category:
Logo
Country:
USA
Year Produced:
1984
Art Director:
Forrest Richardson
Designer:
Forrest Richardson
Design Firm:
Richardson or Richardson
Client:
Christopher Woods Productions

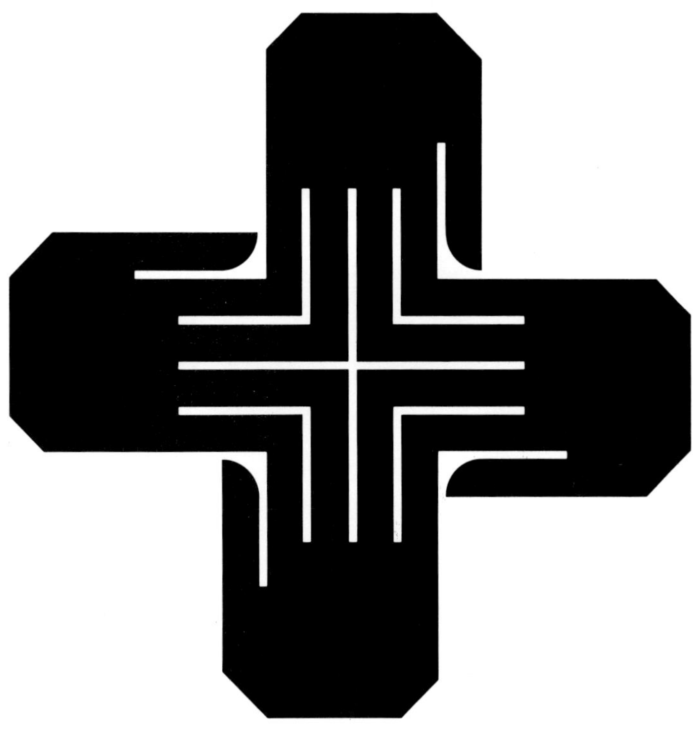

Category:
Logo
Country:
USA
Year Produced:
1989
Art Director:
Kevin Whaley
Designer:
Kevin Whaley
Design Firm:
Grand Pre' & Whaley, Ltd.
Client:
The Area Positive Thinkers

Category:
Logo
Country:
USA
Year Produced:
1985
Art Director:
Josh Freeman
Designer:
Josh Freeman
Design Firm:
Josh Freeman/Associates
Client:
Rancho Encino Hospital

Category:
Logo
Country:
USA
Year Produced:
1980
Art Director:
Jim Berte
Designer:
Vanig Torikian
Design Firm:
Robert Miles Runyan & Associates
Client:
Caremark

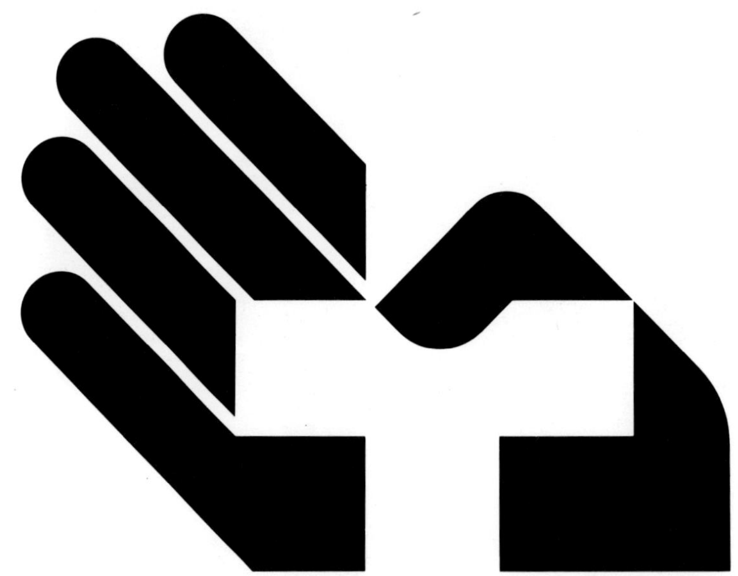

Category:
Stationery
Country:
USA
Year Produced:
1986
Art Director:
Josh Freeman
Designer:
Vickie Sawyer Karten
Design Firm:
Josh Freeman Associates
Client:

Category:
Logo
Country:
Australia
Year Produced:
1980
Art Director:
Annette Harcus and Trevor Crump
Designer:
Annette Harcus
Design Firm:
Annette Harcus Design
Client:
Four In Hand Bar & Restaurant
Illustrator:
Melinda Dudley

Category:
Logo Application
Country:
Australia
Year Produced:
1980
Art Director:
Barrie Tucker
Designer:
Barrie Tucker
Design Firm:
The Fingerprint Company
Client:
The Fingerprint Company

Category:
Stationery
Country:
Australia
Year Produced:
1980
Art Director:
Annette Harcus
Designer:
Annette Harcus
Design Firm:
Annette Harcus Design
Client:
Four in Hand Bar & Restaurant
Illustrator:
Melinda Dudley

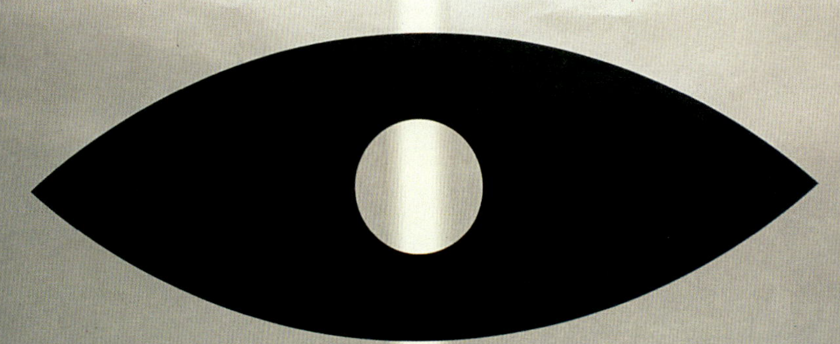
MIDNIGHT JOURNAL

ミッドナイト・ジャーナル
MIDNIGHT JOURNAL
月曜〜金曜 午後11:00放送 キャスター
NHK

Category:
Logo
Country:
Australia
Year Produced:
1988
Art Director:
Annette Harcus
Designer:
Stephanie Martin
Design Firm:
Annette Harcus Design
Client:
Dr. John Elder

Category:
Logo
Country:
USA
Year Produced:
1989
Art Director:
Mickey Moore
Designer:
Mickey Moore
Design Firm:
Mickey Moore Design Associates
Client:
Power Vision

Category:
Logo
Country:
USA
Year Produced:
1988
Art Director:
Keith Bright
Designer:
Raymond Wood and Il Chung
Design Firm:
Bright & Associates
Client:
Eyemasters, Inc.

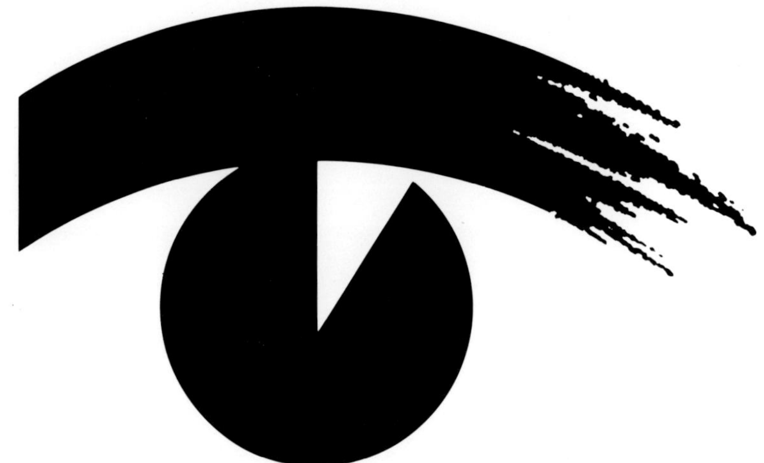

Category:
Logo
Country:
USA
Year Produced:
1989
Art Director:
Margo Chase
Designer:
Margo Chase
Design Firm:
Margo Chase Design
Client:
Sidney Cooper

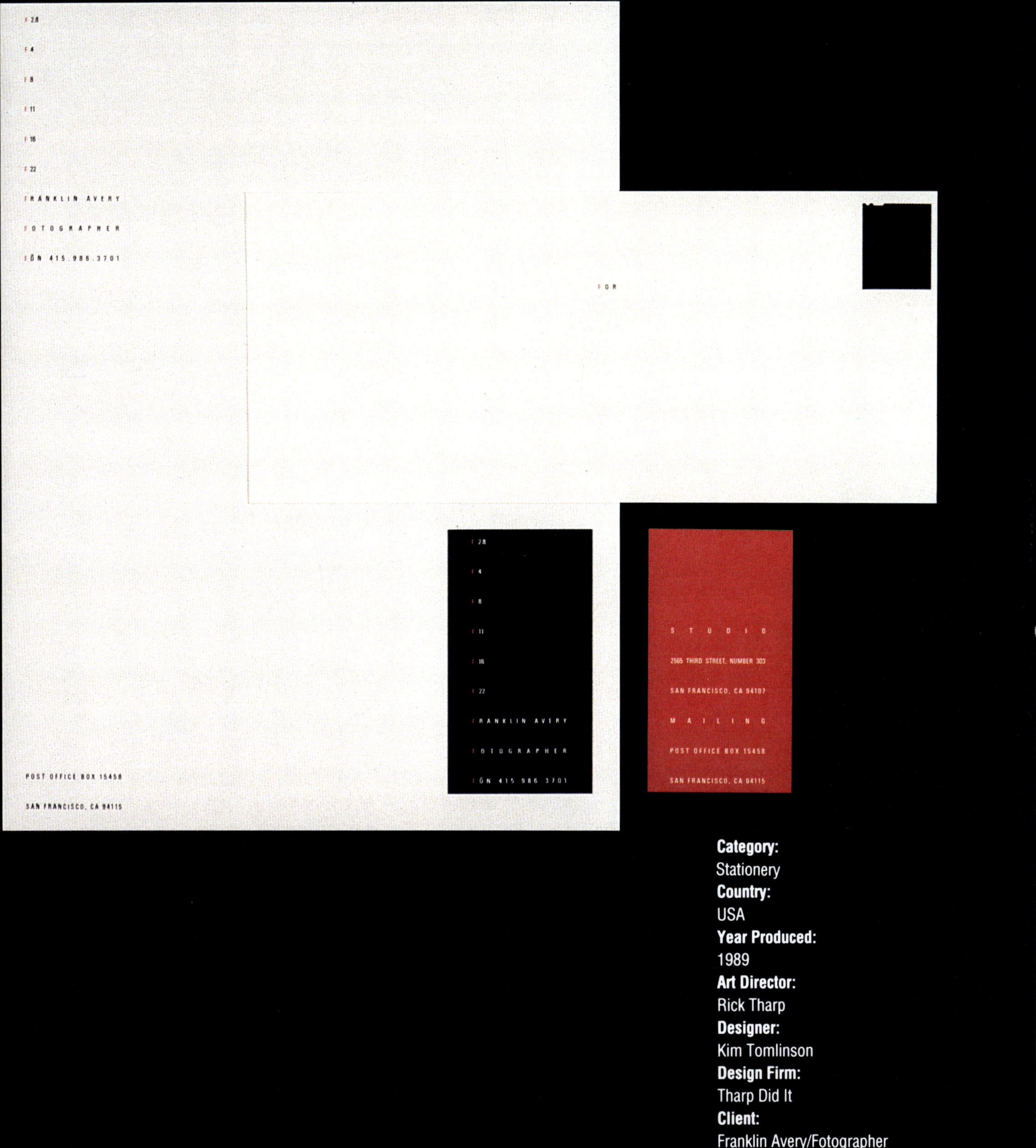

Category:
Stationery
Country:
USA
Year Produced:
1989
Art Director:
Rick Tharp
Designer:
Kim Tomlinson
Design Firm:
Tharp Did It
Client:
Franklin Avery/Fotographer

Category:
Stationery
Country:
USA
Year Produced:
1987
Art Director:
Jack Anderson
Designer:
Jack Anderson and Cheri Huber
Design Firm:
Hornall Anderson Design Works
Client:
Rod Ralston Photography

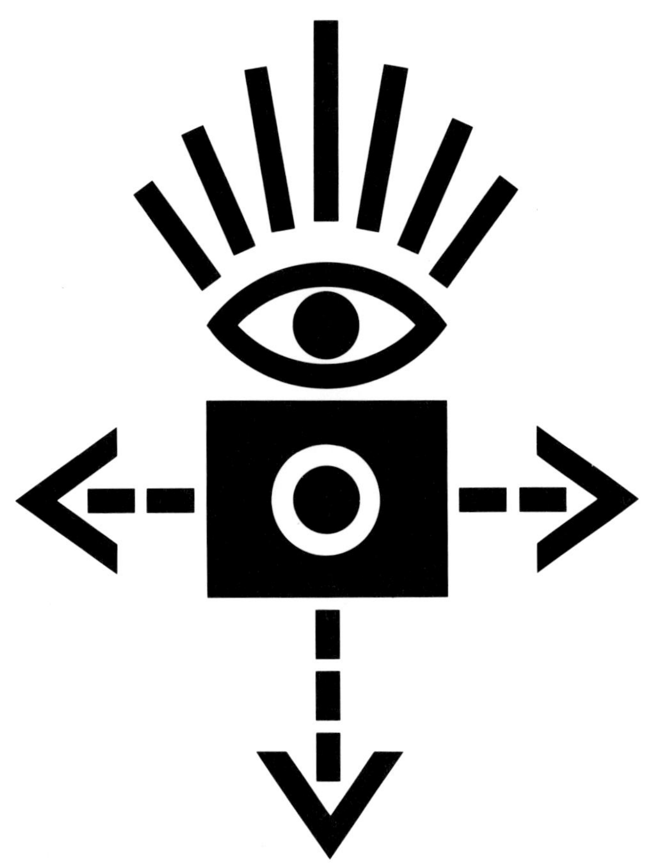

Category:
Logo
Country:
USA
Year Produced:
1989
Art Director:
Planet Design Company
Designer:
Planet Design Company
Design Firm:
Planet Design Company
Client:
Leslie Barton Photography

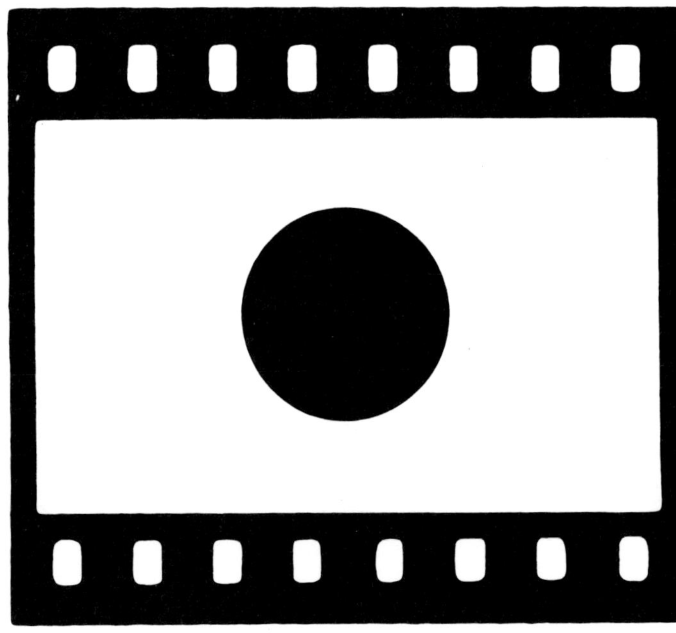

Category:
Logo
Country:
USA
Year Produced:
1981
Art Director:
Jim Lienhart
Designer:
Jim Lienhart
Design Firm:
Murrie Lienhart & Associates
Client:
Peter Sagara Photography

Category:
Logo
Country:
USA
Year Produced:
1986
Art Director:
Joseph M. Dieter, Jr.
Designer:
Joseph M. Dieter, Jr.
Design Firm:
Joseph Dieter Visual Communications
Client:
Joseph Dieter Visual Communications/
Underwater Photography

Category:
Logo
Country:
USA
Year Produced:
1982
Art Director:
Alan Peckolick
Designer:
Alan Peckolick
Design Firm:
Peckolick & Partners
Client:
Warner Communications

Category:
Logo
Country:
USA
Year Produced:
1989
Art Director:
Rusty Kay
Designer:
Susan Rogers
Design Firm:
Rusty Kay & Associates
Client:
Academy of Medical Arts & Sciences

Category:
Logo
Country:
USA
Year Produced:
1983
Art Director:
Gill Fishman
Designer:
David McKutcheon
Design Firm:
Gill Fishman Associates, Inc.
Client:
Jewish Community Center of Boston

Category:
Logo
Country:
USA
Year Produced:
1985
Art Director:
Keith Bright and Larry Klein
Designer:
Raymond Wood
Design Firm:
Bright & Associates
Client:
Los Angeles Olympic Organizing Committee Alumni Organization

Category:
Logo
Country:
USA
Year Produced:
1980
Art Director:
Robert Miles Runyan
Designer:
Jim Berte
Design Firm:
Robert Miles Runyan & Associates
Client:
Los Angeles Olympic Organizing Committee

Category:
Logo Application
Country:
USA
Year Produced:
1986
Art Director:
Kenny Garrison
Designer:
Kenny Garrison
Design Firm:
Richards, Brock, Miller, Mitchell & Associates
Client:
T.G.I. Friday's, Inc.

Category:
Identity Campaign
Country:
USA
Year Produced:
1984
Art Director:
Keith Bright and Larry Klein
Designer:
Raymond Wood and Gretchen Goldie
Design Firm:
Bright & Associates
Client:
Los Angeles Olympic Organizing Committee

Category:
Logo
Country:
USA
Year Produced:
1989
Art Director:
John Evans
Designer:
John Evans
Design Firm:
Sibley/Peteet Design
Client:
Sweatyme

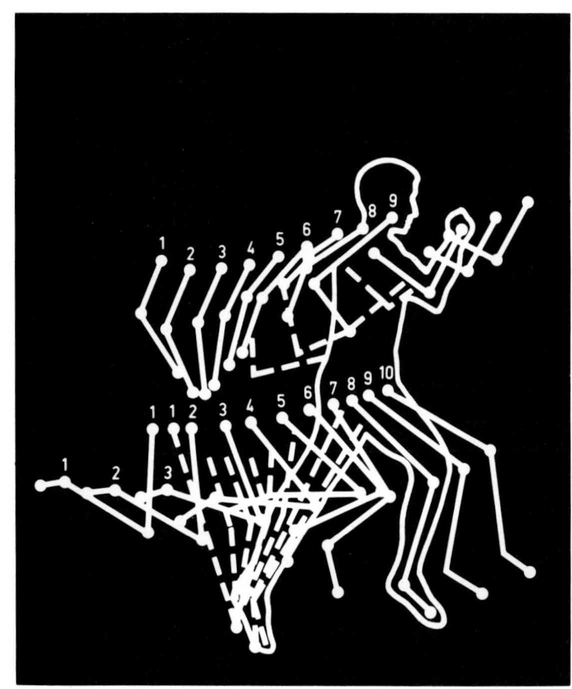

Category:
Logo
Country:
England
Year Produced:
1987
Art Director:
Tor Pettersen
Designer:
David Freeman
Design Firm:
Tor Pettersen & Partners
Client:
March Computer Systems

Category:
Logo
Country:
USA
Year Produced:
1983
Art Director:
Forrest Richardson
Designer:
Forrest Richardson
Design Firm:
Richardson or Richardson
Client:
Phoenix Marathon 1983

Category:
Logo
Country:
USA
Year Produced:
1989
Art Director:
Giulio Turturro
Designer:
Giulio Turturro
Design Firm:
T & A Design
Client:
The Bug Thug

Category:
Logo
Country:
USA
Year Produced:
1985
Art Director:
Jay Vigon and Rick Seireeni
Designer:
Jay Vigon
Design Firm:
Vigon/Seireeni
Client:
Gotcha Sportswear

Category:
Logo Application
Country:
USA
Year Produced:
1989
Art Director:
Mike Salisbury
Designer:
Jay Vigon and Mike Salisbury
Design Firm:
Mike Salisbury Communications, Inc.
Client:
Gotcha Sportswear, Inc.

Category:
Logo
Country:
Australia
Year Produced:
1987
Art Director:
Barrie Tucker
Designer:
Barrie Tucker
Design Firm:
Barrie Tucker Design Pty, Ltd.
Client:
Hilton International Cairns

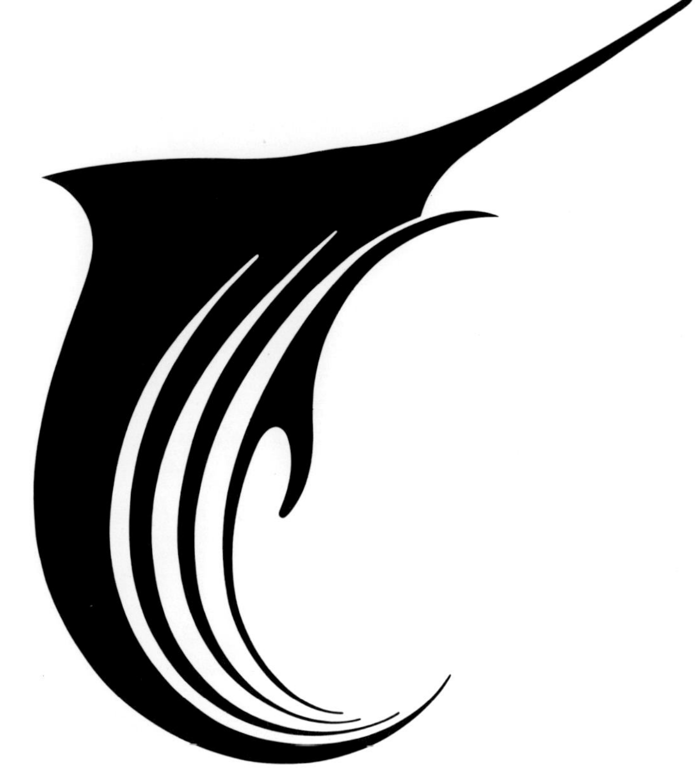

Category:
Logo
Country:
USA
Year Produced:
1989
Art Director:
Rusty Kay
Designer:
Susan Rogers
Design Firm:
Rusty Kay & Associates
Client:
Fish Company

Category:
Packaging
Country:
USA
Year Produced:
1988
Art Director:
Nicolas Sidjakov and Jerry Berman
Designer:
Tom McNulty
Design Firm:
SBG Partners
Client:
Fintek, Inc.
Illustrator:
Justin Carroll

Category:
Packaging
Country:
USA
Year Produced:
1986
Art Director:
Jerry Berman and Nicolas Sidjakov
Designer:
Barbara Vick and Courtney Reeser
Design Firm:
SBG Partners
Client:
Berkley, Inc.
Illustrator:
Will Nelson

Category:
Logo
Country:
USA
Year Produced:
1989
Art Director:
Jay Vigon
Designer:
Jay Vigon
Design Firm:
Jay Vigon
Client:
Sharkfin

Category:
Logo
Country:
USSR
Year Produced:
1980
Art Director:
Marat Bejajev
Designer:
Marat Bejajev
Design Firm:
Sobyetvienost Avtora
Client:
Marat Bejajev

Category:
Logo
Country:
Hong Kong
Year Produced:
1989
Art Director:
Kan Tai-keung
Designer:
Freeman Lau Siu-hong
Design Firm:
Kan Tai-keung Design & Associates, Ltd.
Client:
Frog & Associates, Inc.

青蛙出版社
Frog & Associates Inc.
青蛙出版社
青蛙出版社
青蛙出版社
Frog (Far East) Press
Central · Hong Kong
Frog & Associates Inc.
Frog (Far East) Press
Frog Publishing
Frog Distribution

Category:

Category:
Logo
Country:
USA
Year Produced:
1981
Art Director:
Marilyn Worseldine
Designer:
Marilyn Worseldine
Design Firm:
Market Sights, Inc.
Client:
Big Black Chicken

Category:
Logo
Country:
Germany
Year Produced:
1984
Art Director:
Heinz Kippnick
Designer:
Heinz Kippnick
Design Firm:
Gebrauchsgrafiker VBK
Client:
Schweriner Folklore

Category:
Logo
Country:
USA
Year Produced:
1981
Art Director:
Ryo Urano
Designer:
Ryo Urano
Design Firm:
Urano Communication International
Client:
Unity School

Category:
Logo
Country:
USSR
Year Produced:
1980
Art Director:
Marat Bejajev
Designer:
Marat Bejajev
Design Firm:
Sobyetvienost Avtora
Client:
Marat Bejajev

Category:
Logo
Country:
Canada
Year Produced:
1987
Art Director:
Gus Tsetsekas
Designer:
Gus Tsetsekas and Mark Friesen
Design Firm:
Signals Design Group, Inc.
Client:
Canadian Helicopters

Category:
Logo
Country:
England
Year Produced:
1989
Art Director:
John Larkin
Designer:
Katie Arup
Design Firm:
Design House
Client:
Goldcrest Films

Category:
Logo
Country:
USA
Year Produced:
1989
Art Director:
Courtney Reeser
Designer:
Jackie Foshaug
Design Firm:
SBG Partners
Client:
Paccar Parts

Category:
Logo
Country:
USA
Year Produced:
1987
Art Director:
Rex Peteet
Designer:
Julia Albanesi
Design Firm:
Sibley/Peteet Design
Client:
Melvin Simon

Category:
Logo
Country:
England
Year Produced:
1988
Art Director:
Karen Blincoe
Designer:
Karen Blincoe and Richard Fisher-Smith
Design Firm:
KB Design
Client:
Pegasus Print & Display, Ltd.

Category:
Logo
Country:
USA
Year Produced:
1987
Art Director:
Suzanne Miller
Designer:
Suzanne Miller
Design Firm:
Suzanne Miller Design
Client:
U.C. Berkeley (Bears) Fencing Team

Date

Ref

Your Ref

PEGASUS

Pegasus Print and Display Limited
10 Osier Way
Mitcham Surrey CR4 4NF
Telephone 01 640 1201/2/3
and 01 640 6521/2
Facsimile 01 640 2781
Registered in England No 977135

Category:
Logo Application
Country:
England
Year Produced:
1988
Art Director:
Karen Blincoe
Designer:
Karen Blincoe and Richard Fisher-Smith
Design Firm:
KB Design
Client:
Pegasus Print & Display, Ltd.

Category:
Logo
Country:
USA
Year Produced:
1989
Art Director:
Stephen Miller
Designer:
Stephen Miller
Design Firm:
Richards, Brock, Miller, Mitchell & Associates
Client:
Oryx Energy Company

Category:
Logo
Country:
Canada
Year Produced:
1989
Art Director:
Amanda Finn
Designer:
Amanda Finn
Design Firm:
Lawrence Finn & Associates, Ltd.
Client:
B.B.II Importers, Inc.

Category:
Logo
Country:
USA
Year Produced:
1988
Art Director:
Rex Peteet
Designer:
Rex Peteet
Design Firm:
Sibley/Peteet Design
Client:
Mesa

Category:
Logo
Country:
USA
Year Produced:
1987
Art Director:
Giulio Turturro
Designer:
Giulio Turturro
Design Firm:
T & A Design
Client:
U.S. Postal Service

Category:
Logo
Country:
USA
Year Produced:
1980
Art Director:
Lance Wyman
Designer:
Lance Wyman
Design Firm:
Lance Wyman, Ltd.
Client:
Minnesota Zoo

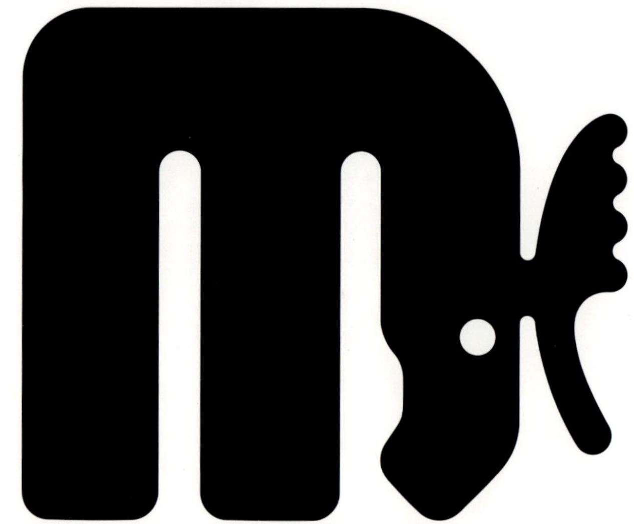

Category:
Identity Campaign
Country:
USA
Year Produced:
1980
Art Director:
Lance Wyman
Designer:
Lance Wyman, Stephen Schlott and
Linda Iskander
Design Firm:
Lance Wyman, Ltd.
Client:
Minnesota Zoo

ONE
WAY

Category:
Logo
Country:
USA
Year Produced:
1988
Art Director:
Woody Pirtle
Designer:
Penny Rowland
Design Firm:
Pentagram
Client:
Fox River Paper

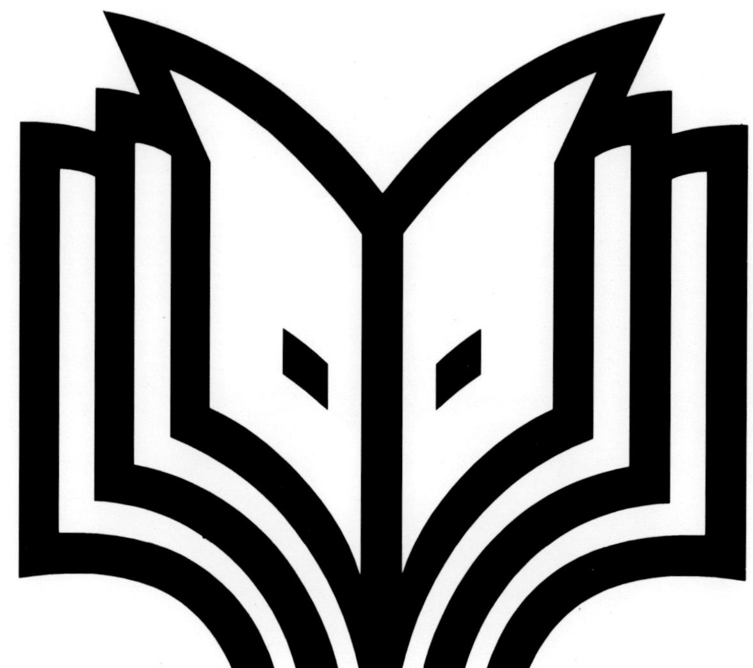

Category:
Logo
Country:
Japan
Year Produced:
1989
Art Director:
Shin Matsunaga
Designer:
Shin Matsunaga
Design Firm:
Shin Matsunaga Design, Inc.
Client:
Ajinomoto General Foods, Inc.

Category:
Logo
Country:
USA
Year Produced:
1987
Art Director:
Michael Toth
Designer:
Michael Schwab
Design Firm:
Michael Schwab Design
Client:
Robert Bruce Sweaters

Category:
Logo
Country:
USA
Year Produced:
1984
Art Director:
Jay Vigon and Rick Seireeni
Designer:
Jay Vigon
Design Firm:
Vigon/Seireeni
Client:
Creative Planet

Category:
Logo
Country:
USA
Year Produced:
1987
Art Director:
Nicolas Sidjakov and Jerry Berman
Designer:
Ben Wheeler
Design Firm:
SBG Partners
Client:
Aussie Enterprises

Category:
Logo
Country:
USA
Year Produced:
1988
Art Director:
Ken Shafer
Designer:
Ken Shafer
Design Firm:
Richards, Brock, Miller, Mitchell
& Associates
Client:
Team Mad Dog

Category:
Logo
Country:
USA
Year Produced:
1987
Art Director:
David Beck
Designer:
David Beck
Design Firm:
Sibley/Peteet Design
Client:
Texas Association for Stolen Children

Category:
Logo
Country:
Germany
Year Produced:
1986
Art Director:
Lothar Freund
Designer:
Lothar Freund
Design Firm:
Lothar Freund
Client:
Lothar Freund

Category:
Logo
Country:
USA
Year Produced:
1989
Art Director:
C. Baldwin, R. Raye and
M. Strassburger
Designer:
Christopher Baldwin
Design Firm:
Modern Dog
Client:
Modern Dog

Category:
Logo
Country:
USA
Year Produced:
1986
Art Director:
Luis D. Acevedo
Designer:
Luis D. Acevedo
Design Firm:
Richards, Brock, Miller, Mitchell
& Associates
Client:
Lewisville Humane Society

Trajna delovna skupnost samostojnih kulturnih delavcev FENIKS p.o.
61000 Ljubljana, Mestni trg 10, Slovenija, Jugoslavija 061/212-972

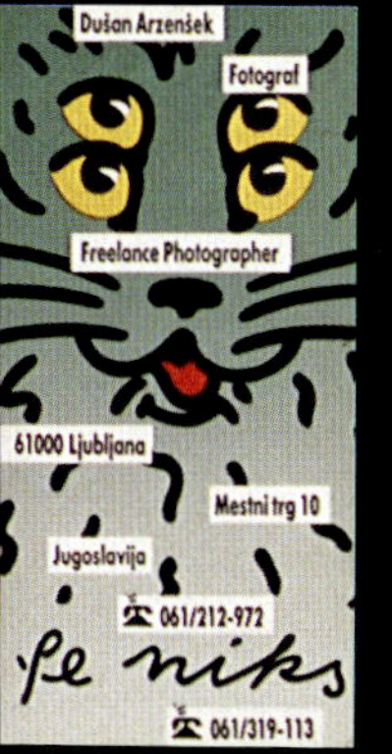

Category:
Identity Capaign
Country:
Yugoslavia
Year Produced:
1987
Art Director:
Radovan Jenko
Designer:
Radovan Jenko
Design Firm:
Visual Communications
Client:

Category:
Logo
Country:
USA
Year Produced:
1983
Art Director:
Dick Mitchell
Designer:
Dick Mitchell
Design Firm:
Richards, Brock, Miller, Mitchell & Associates
Client:
The Dallas Zoo

Category:
Logo
Country:
Canada
Year Produced:
1981
Art Director:
Neville Smith
Designer:
Neville Smith
Design Firm:
Neville Smith Graphic Design
Client:
Black Cat Cafe

Category:
Logo Application
Country:
Denmark
Year Produced:
1980
Art Director:
Poul K. Andersen
Designer:
Finn Simonsen
Design Firm:
Siegel & Gale A/S
Client:
Sonderborg Garn

Category:
Logo
Country:
USA
Year Produced:
1988
Art Director:
Bill Gardner
Designer:
Bill Gardner
Design Firm:
Gardner-Greteman-Mikulecky
Client:
Wichita Cat Hospital

Category:
Logo
Country:
USA
Year Produced:
1984
Art Director:
Steve Snider
Designer:
Steve Snider
Design Firm:
Snider Design
Client:
Richman's Zipper Hospital

Category:
Logo
Country:
USA
Year Produced:
1986
Art Director:
Ellen Shapiro
Designer:
Ellen Shapiro
Design Firm:
Shapiro Design Associates, Inc.
Client:
United Hospital Fund

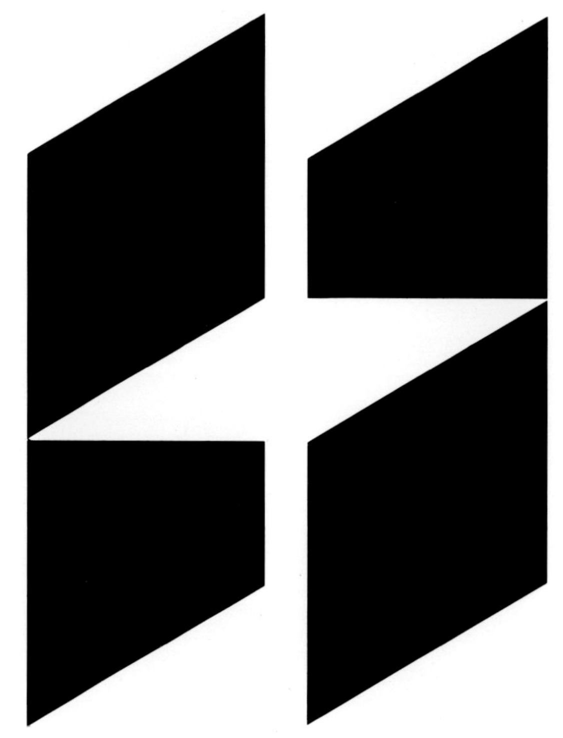

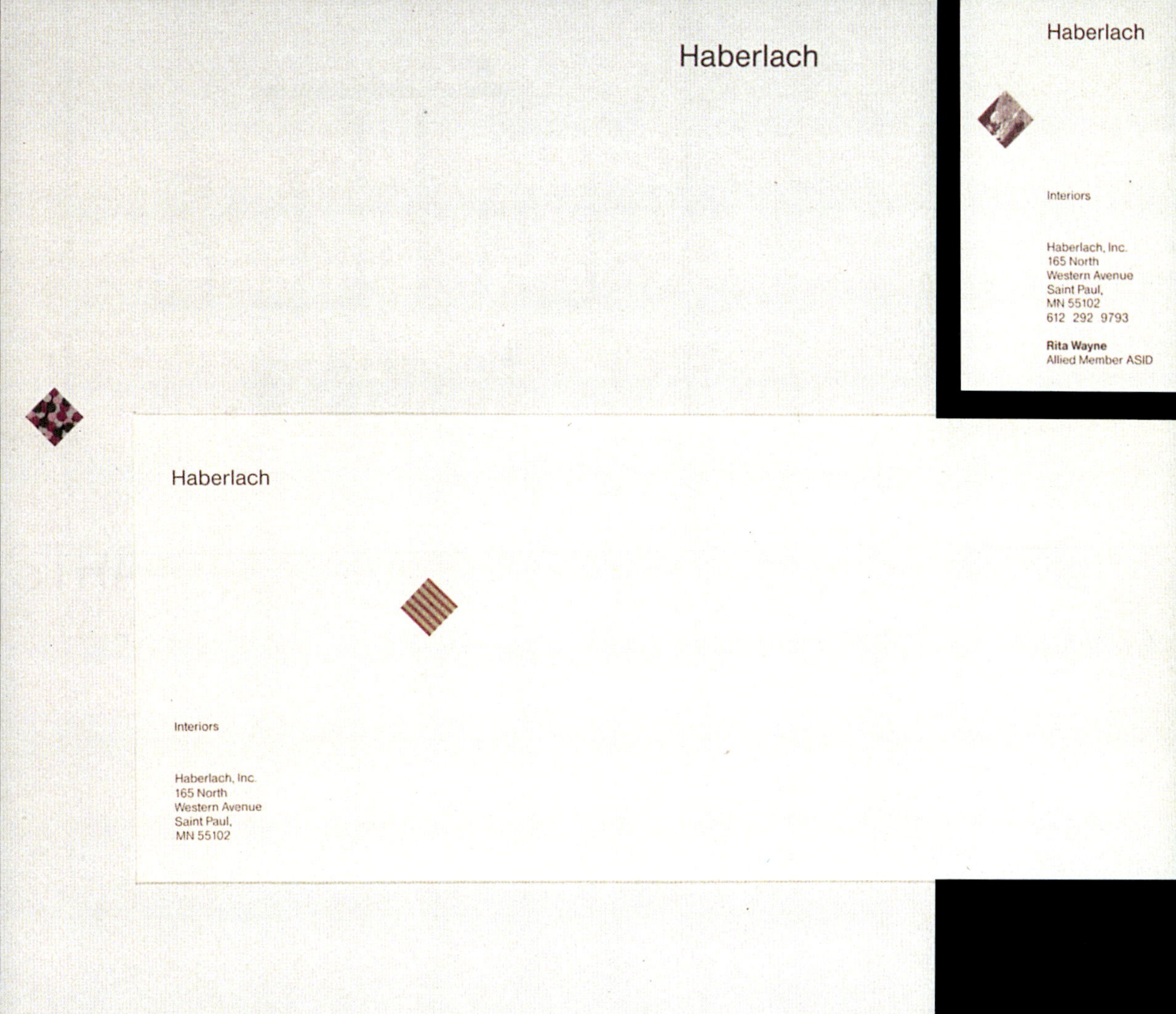

Category:
Stationery
Country:
USA
Year Produced:
1988
Art Director:
Bruce Rubin
Designer:
John Haines
Design Firm:
Rubin Cordaro Design
Client:
Haberlach, Inc.

Category:
Logo
Country:
USA
Year Produced:
1987
Art Director:
Bruce Yelaska
Designer:
Bruce Yelaska
Design Firm:
Bruce Yelaska Design
Client:
Little City Restaurant & Antipasti Bar

Category:
Logo
Country:
USA
Year Produced:
1985
Art Director:
D.C. Stipp
Designer:
D.C. Stipp
Design Firm:
Richards, Brock, Miller, Mitchell
& Associates
Client:
Cabinetree Cabinet Shop

CABINETREE

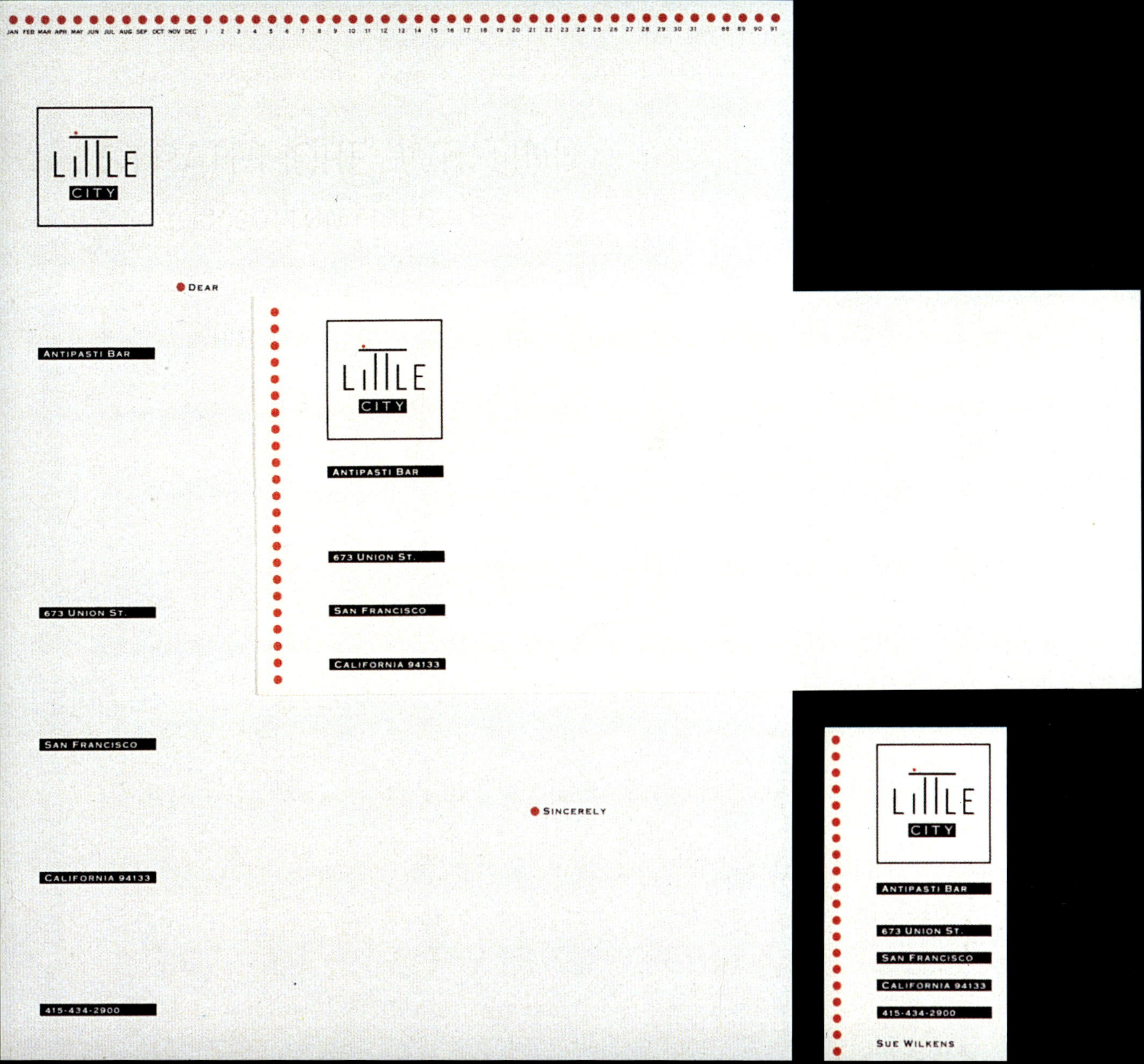

LITTLE CITY

DEAR

ANTIPASTI BAR

673 UNION ST.

SAN FRANCISCO

SINCERELY

CALIFORNIA 94133

415-434-2900

LITTLE CITY

ANTIPASTI BAR

673 UNION ST.

SAN FRANCISCO

CALIFORNIA 94133

Category:
Stationery
Country:
USA
Year Produced:
1987
Art Director:
Bruce Yelaska
Designer:
Bruce Yelaska
Design Firm:
Bruce Yelaska Design
Client:

MERLETTO

425½ N. Rodeo Drive, Rodeo Collection, Beverly Hills, CA 90210
Telephone: (213) 273-1038

Category:
Stationery
Country:
Canada
Year Produced:
1989
Art Director:
Amanda Finn
Designer:
Amanda Finn
Design Firm:
Lawrence Finn & Associates, Ltd.

Monica Alamán Lagarcé

425½ N. Rodeo Drive, Rodeo Collection, Beverly Hills, CA 90210
Telephone: (213) 273-1038

Category:
Stationery
Country:
USA
Year Produced:
1985 & 1988
Art Director:
Peter Harrison
Designer:
Susan Hochbaum
Design Firm:
Pentagram
Client:
The '21' Club

Category:
Stationery
Country:
USA
Year Produced:
1985
Art Director:
Rick Tharp
Designer:
Rick Tharp and Kimi Nomura
Design Firm:
Tharp Did It
Client:
Tharp Did It

Category:
Logo
Country:
USA
Year Produced:
1989
Art Director:
Tamotsu Yagi
Designer:
Tamotsu Yagi
Design Firm:
Esprit Graphic Design Studio
Client:
Esprit

Category:
Logo
Country:
Japan
Year Produced:
1986
Art Director:
Helmut Schmid
Designer:
Helmut Schmid
Design Firm:
Helmut Schmid Design
JMS International/PAI
Client:
itariyard

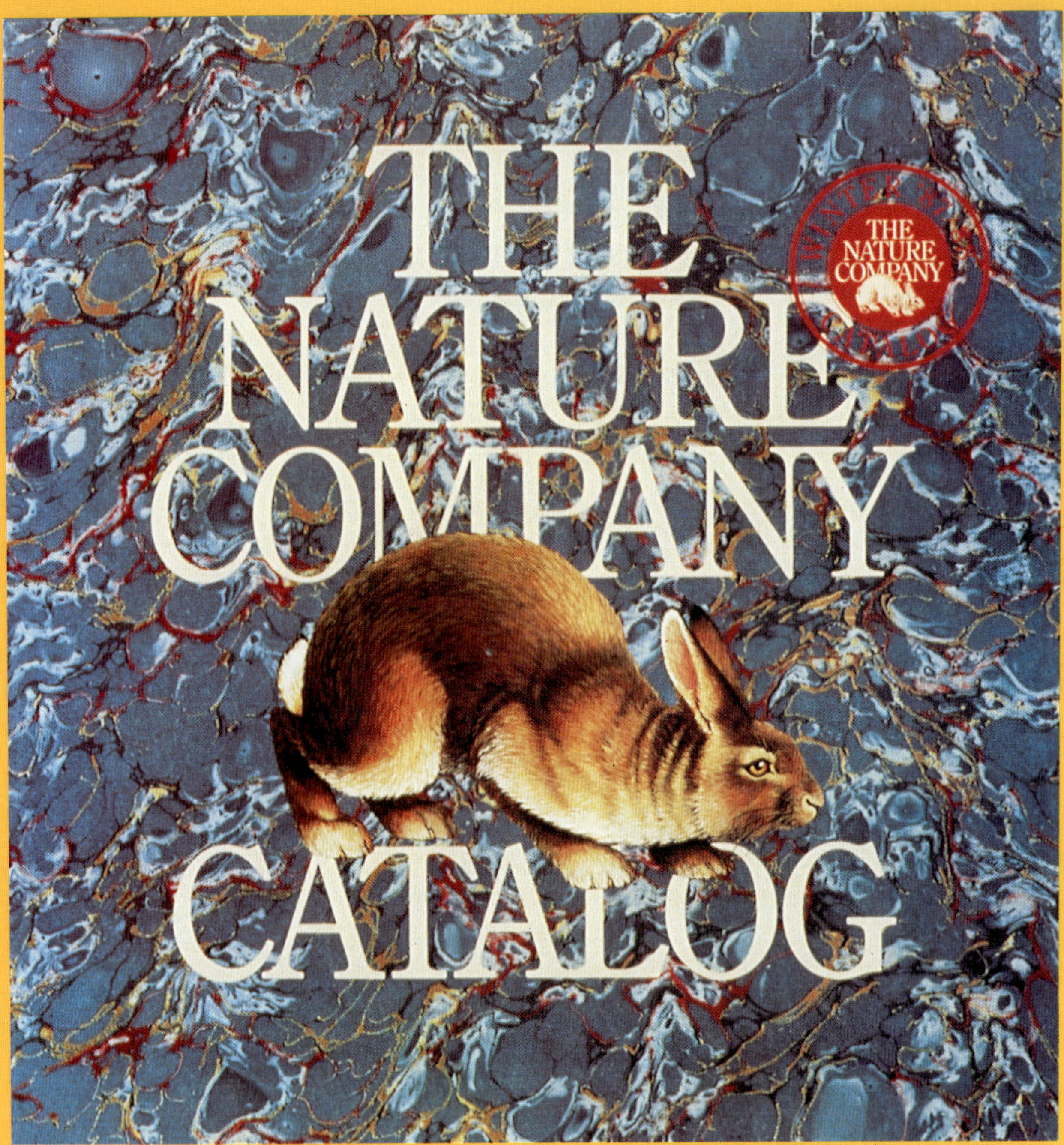

Category:
Logo Application
Country:
USA
Year Produced:
1987
Art Director:
Kit Hinrichs
Designer:
Kit Hinrichs and Natalie Kitamura
Design Firm:
Pentagram
Client:
The Nature Company

Category:
Packaging
Country:
USA
Year Produced:
1989
Art Director:
Courtney Reeser
Designer:
Courtney Reeser
Design Firm:
SBG Partners
Client:
Williams-Sonoma
Copywriter:
Donata Maggipinto

Category:
Logo
Country:
USA
Year Produced:
1989
Art Director:
Conrad Jorgensen
Designer:
Mary Brucken
Design Firm:
SBG Partners
Client:
Kobacker Fashion Affiliates

Category:
Logo
Country:
USA
Year Produced:
1988
Art Director:
Tim Thompson
Designer:
Joe Parisi
Design Firm:
Graffito
Client:
Oriole System Software

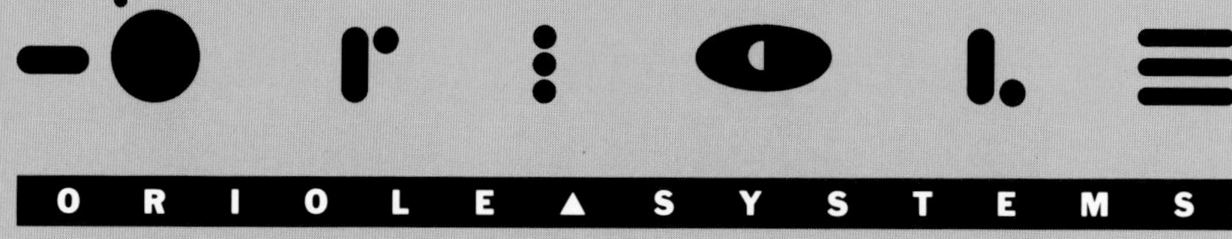

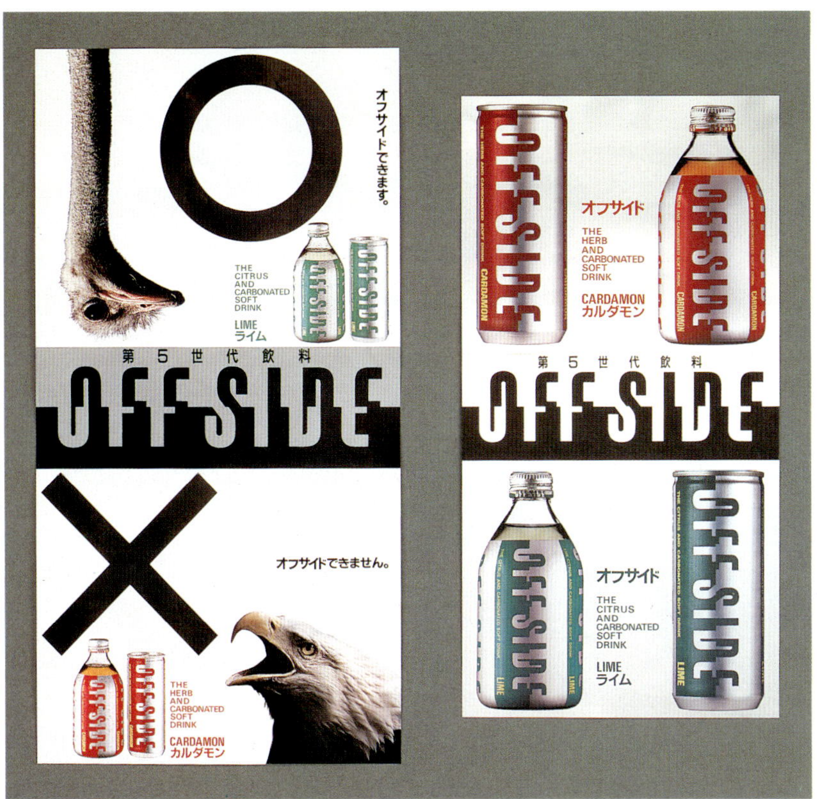

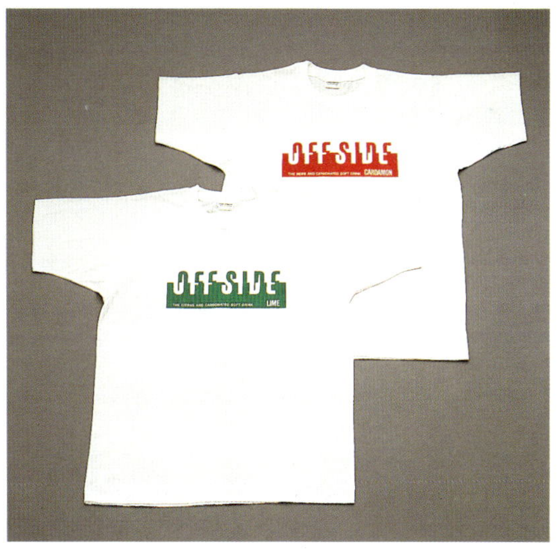

Category:
Identity Campaign
Country:
Japan
Year Produced:
1980
Art Director:
Shigeo Katsuoka
Designer:
Shigeo Katsuoka
Design Firm:
Shigeo Katsuoka Design Studio
Client:
Kirin Brewery Company, Ltd.

Category:
Logo
Country:
Canada
Year Produced:
1989
Art Director:
Tiit Telmet
Designer:
Joseph Gault and Tiit Telmet
Design Firm:
Telmet Design Associates
Client:
Dance Umbrella of Ontario

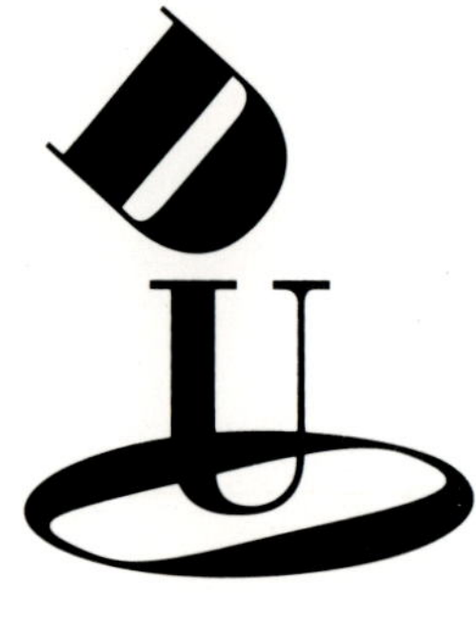

Category:
Logo
Country:
Australia
Year Produced:
1989
Art Director:
Annette Harcus
Designer:
Stephanie Martin
Design Firm:
Annette Harcus Design
Client:
Film Australia Pty, Ltd.

DANCE
UMBRELLA OF
ONTARIO

DANCE
UMBRELLA OF
ONTARIO

553 QUEEN STREET WEST, SUITE 400
TORONTO, ONTARIO M5V 2B6
TEL 416 360-6429 FAX 416 363-8702

Category:
Stationery
Country:
Canada
Year Produced:
1989
Art Director:
Tiit Telmet
Designer:
Joseph Gault and Tiit Telmet
Design Firm:
Telmet Design Associates
Client:
Dance Umbrella of Ontario

Category:
Logo
Country:
USA
Year Produced:
1989
Art Director:
Primo Angeli
Designer:
Philippe Becker and Ray Honda
Design Firm:
Primo Angeli, Inc.
Client:
Just Desserts

Category:
Logo
Country:
USA
Year Produced:
1989
Art Director:
Rolando Rosler
Designer:
Rolando Rosler, Ian McLean and Mark Crumpacker
Design Firm:
Primo Angeli, Inc.
Client:
Lavazza
Creative Director:
Primo Angeli

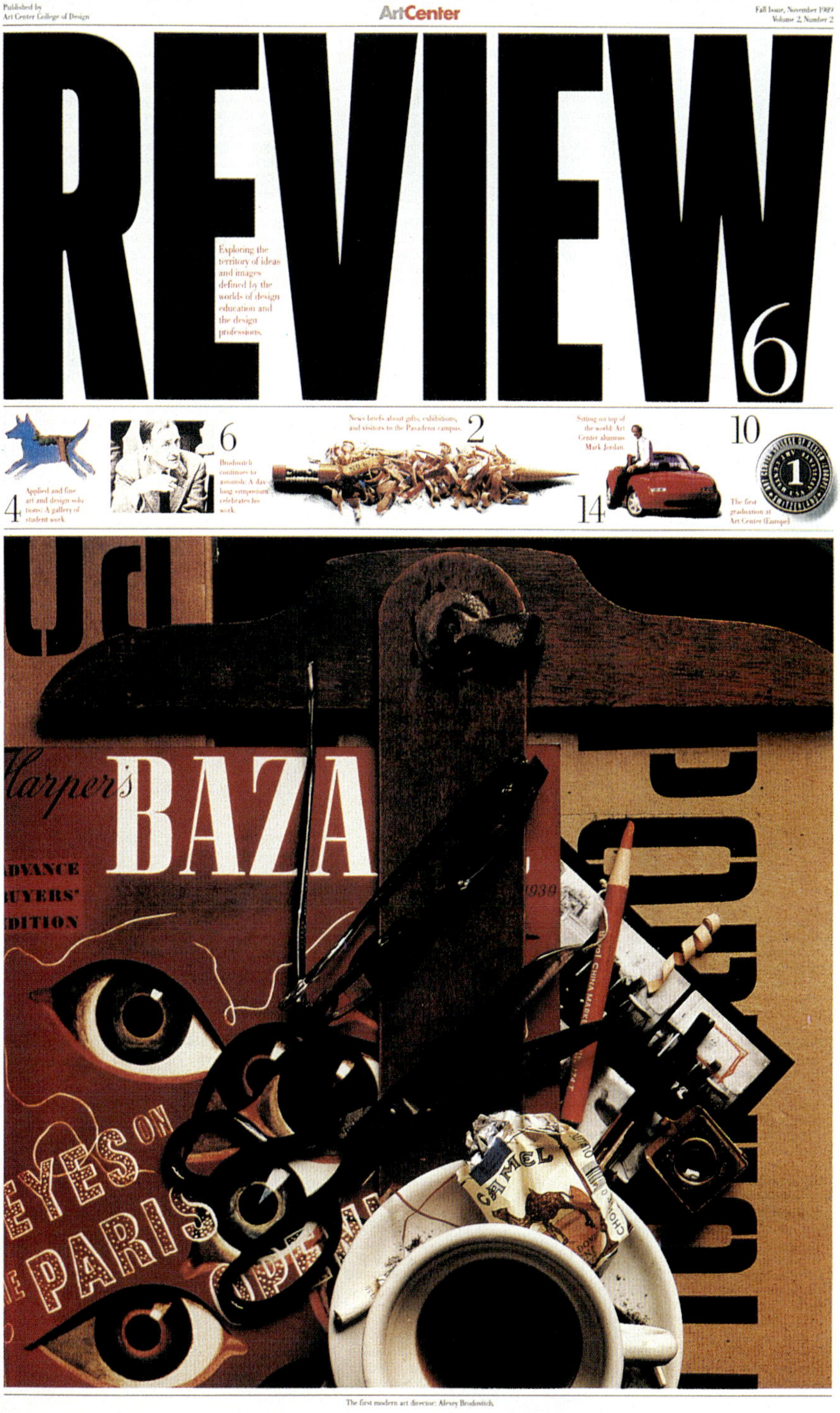

The first modern art director: Alexey Brodovitch.

Category:
Logo Application
Country:
USA
Year Produced:
1989
Art Director:
Kit Hinrichs
Designer:
Kit Hinrichs and Terri Driscoll
Design Firm:
Pentagram
Client:
Art Center College of Design

Category:
Logo
Country:
USA
Year Produced:
1987
Art Director:
Gordon Mortensen
Designer:
Gordon Mortensen
Design Firm:
Mortensen Design
Client:
Radius, Inc.

radius

Category:
Packaging
Country:
USA
Year Produced:
1987
Art Director:
Gordon Mortensen
Designer:
Gordon Mortensen
Design Firm:
Mortensen Design
Client:
Radius, Inc..
Copywriter:
Barbara Gibson

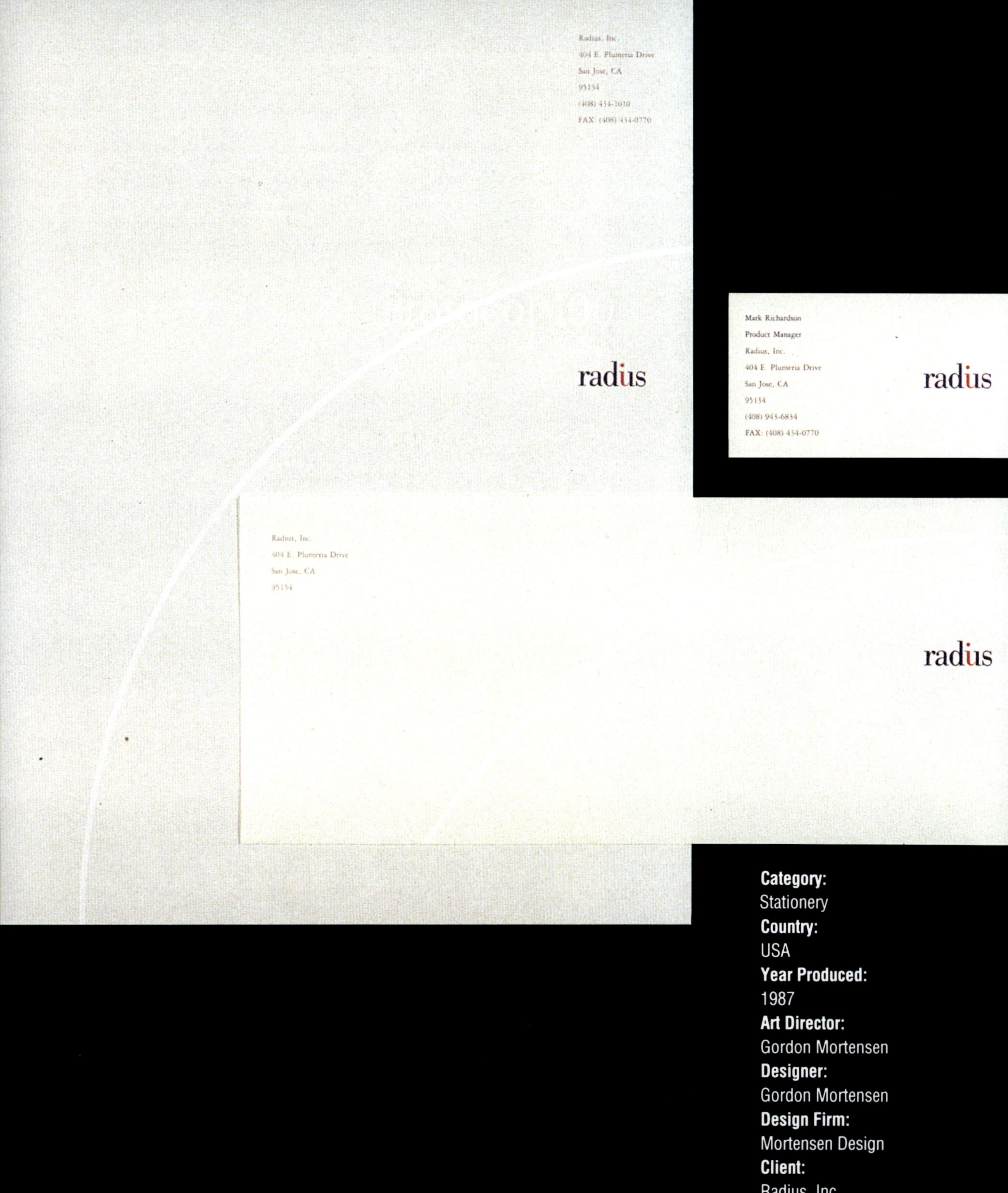

Category:
Stationery
Country:
USA
Year Produced:
1987
Art Director:
Gordon Mortensen
Designer:
Gordon Mortensen
Design Firm:
Mortensen Design
Client:
Radius, Inc.

Category:
Logo
Country:
USA
Year Produced:
1989
Art Director:
Tamotsu Yagi
Designer:
Tamotsu Yagi
Design Firm:
Esprit Graphic Design Studio
Client:
Esprit City T-shirt

Category:
Logo
Country:
USA
Year Produced:
1989
Art Director:
Tamotsu Yagi
Designer:
Tamotsu Yagi
Design Firm:
Esprit Graphic Design Studio
Client:
Esprit Amish Quilt T-shirt

LUCY'S LACES™

Category:
Logo
Country:
USA
Year Produced:
1983
Art Director:
Gill Fishman
Designer:
Jeff Kennedy
Design Firm:
Gill Fishman Associates, Inc.
Client:
Lucy's Laces

BUMBLE+BUMBLE

Category:
Logo
Country:
USA
Year Produced:
1985
Art Director:
Mike Quon and M. Gordon
Designer:
Mike Quon
Design Firm:
Mike Quon Design Office
Client:
Bumble+Bumble, Inc.

Category:
Logo
Country:
USA
Year Produced:
1986
Art Director:
Daniel Ruesch
Designer:
Daniel Ruesch
Design Firm:
Tandem Studios
Client:
Utah Associated Municipal Power Systems

Category:
Logo
Country:
USA
Year Produced:
1989
Art Director:
Kym Abrams
Designer:
Mike Stees
Design Firm:
Kym Abrams Design
Client:
G.J. Nikolas & Company

deci.mal

Category:
Logo
Country:
USA
Year Produced:
1985
Art Director:
Samuel Kuo
Designer:
Samuel Kuo
Design Firm:
Samuel Kuo Design
Client:
The Society of Librarians

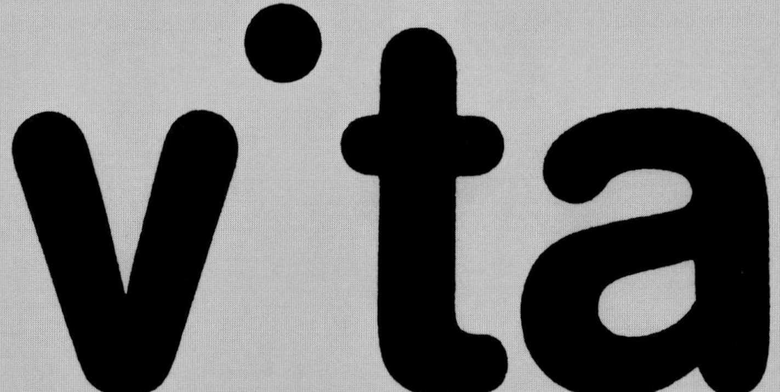

Category:
Logo
Country:
Switzerland
Year Produced:
1986
Art Director:
Michael Baviera
Designer:
Michael Baviera
Design Firm:
BBV
Client:
Vita Insurance Company

Category:
Logo
Country:
Canada
Year Produced:
1985
Art Director:
Christian Labarthe
Designer:
Christian Labarthe
Design Firm:
Wawa Design
Client:
Tovind Consulting, Inc.

Category:
Logo
Country:
USA
Year Produced:
1988
Art Director:
Margo Chase
Designer:
Lorna Stovall
Design Firm:
Margo Chase Design
Client:
Virgin Records America, Inc.

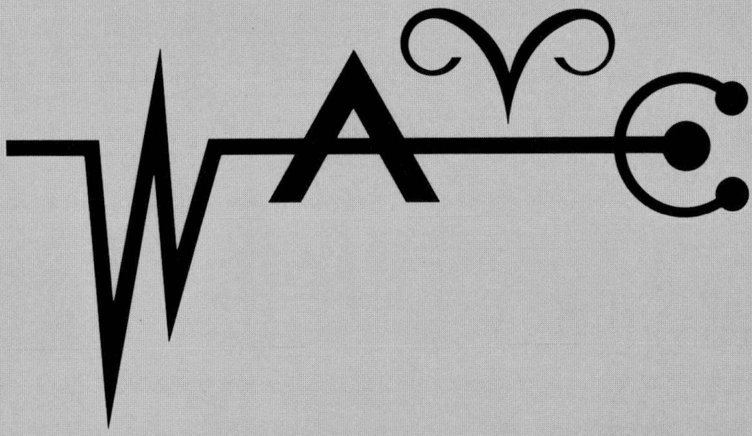

Category:
Logo
Country:
USA
Year Produced:
1987
Art Director:
Jay Vigon and Rick Seireeni
Designer:
Jay Vigon
Design Firm:
Vigon/Seireeni
Client:
Wave Restaurant

OCTAS
90

Category:
Logo
Country:
Canada
Year Produced:
1989
Art Director:
Marie Rodrigue
Designer:
Marie Rodrigue
Design Firm:
Verge LeBel Communication, Inc.
Client:
Federation Informatique de Quebec

Category:
Packaging
Country:
Japan
Year Produced:
1986
Art Director:
Shin Matsunaga
Designer:
Shin Matsunaga
Design Firm:
Shin Matsunaga Design, Inc.
Client:
Sanyo Scott Company, Ltd.

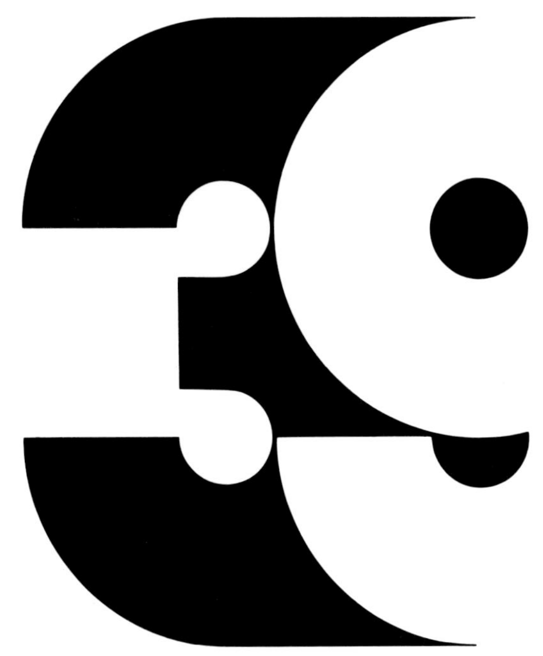

Category:
Logo
Country:
USA
Year Produced:
1983
Art Director:
Jim Frazier, Don Sibley and Rex Peteet
Designer:
Walter Horton
Design Firm:
Sibley/Peteet Design
Client:
Arnold, Harwell & McClain/KXTX 39

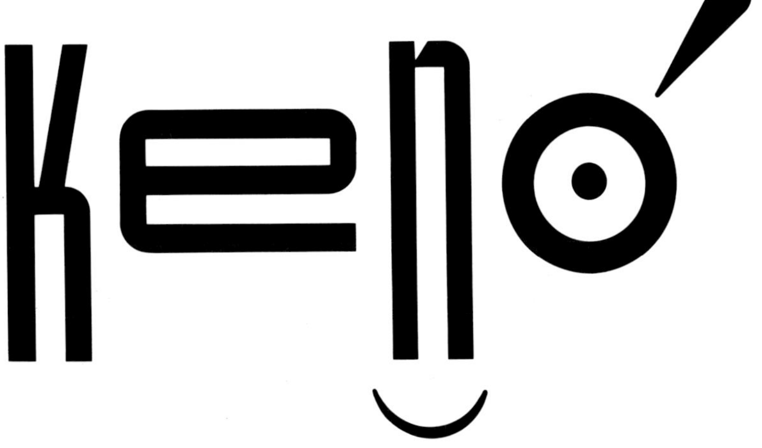

Category:
Logo
Country:
USA
Year Produced:
1989
Art Director:
Tim Lachowski and Donna McGuire
Designer:
Donna McGuire
Design Firm:
Primadonna
Client:
Michigan State Lottery

Category:
Logo Application
Country:
Netherlands
Year Produced:
1989
Art Director:
Andre Toet
Designer:
Andre Toet
Design Firm:
Samenwerkende Ontwerpers
Client:
Dagbladunie
Photography:
Tjeerd Frederikse

5989A South Loop East Houston, Texas 77033 (713) 644-1018

5989A South Loop East Houston, Texas 77033 (713) 644-1018

Category:
Stationery
Country:
USA
Year Produced:
1985
Art Director:
Abraham J. Amuny
Designer:
Abraham J. Amuny
Design Firm:
Art City Corporation
Client:
Art City Corporation
Photographer:
George Craig
Airbrush Artist:
Jeff Sanson

Category:
Logo
Country:
USA
Year Produced:
1987
Art Director:
Margo Chase
Designer:
Margo Chase
Design Firm:
Margo Chase Design
Client:
Motown Records

Category:
Logo
Country:
USA
Year Produced:
1982
Art Director:
Richard Listenberger
Designer:
Richard Listenberger
Design Firm:
Listenberger Design Associates
Client:
International Violin Competition of Indianapolis

Category:
Logo
Country:
USA
Year Produced:
1986
Art Director:
Alex Jay
Designer:
Alex Jay
Design Firm:
Studio J
Client:
Wendy O. Williams

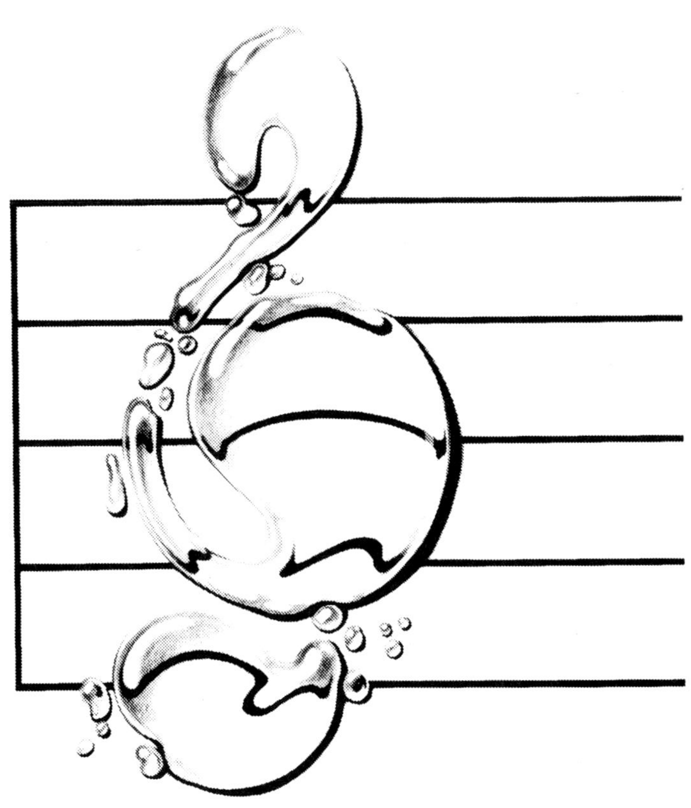

Category:
Logo
Country:
USA
Year Produced:
1980
Art Director:
Gill Fishman
Designer:
Gill Fishman
Design Firm:
Gill Fishman Associates, Inc.
Client:
Water Music
Illustrator:
Paul Levy

Category:
Logo
Country:
USA
Year Produced:
1986
Art Director:
Don Sibley
Designer:
John Evans
Design Firm:
Sibley/Peteet Design
Client:
Mickey Newbury

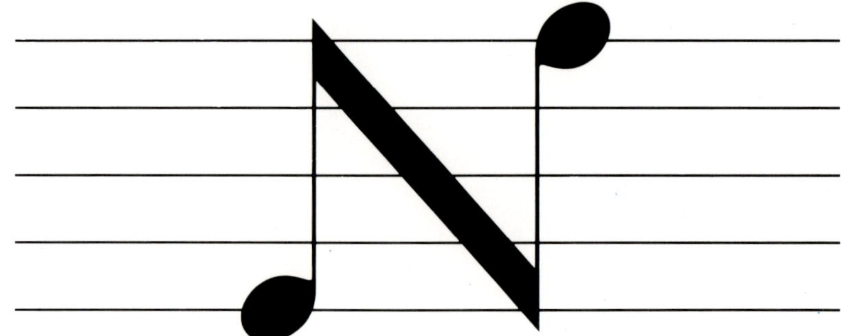

Category:
Logo Application
Country:
USA
Year Produced:
1986
Art Director:
Don Sibley and John Evans
Designer:
John Evans
Design Firm:
Sibley/Peteet Design
Client:
Mickey Newbury

Category:
Stationery
Country:
USA
Year Produced:
1986
Art Director:
Don Sibley and John Evans

Category:
Logo
Country:
USA
Year Produced:
1985
Art Director:
Rex Peteet and Walter Horton
Designer:
Rex Peteet and Walter Horton
Design Firm:
Sibley/Peteet Design
Client:
Trammell Crow/Amadeus Restaurant

Category:
Logo
Country:
USA
Year Produced:
1984
Art Director:
Mike Zender
Designer:
Mike Zender
Design Firm:
Zender+Associates, Inc.
Client:
Cincinnati Composers Guild

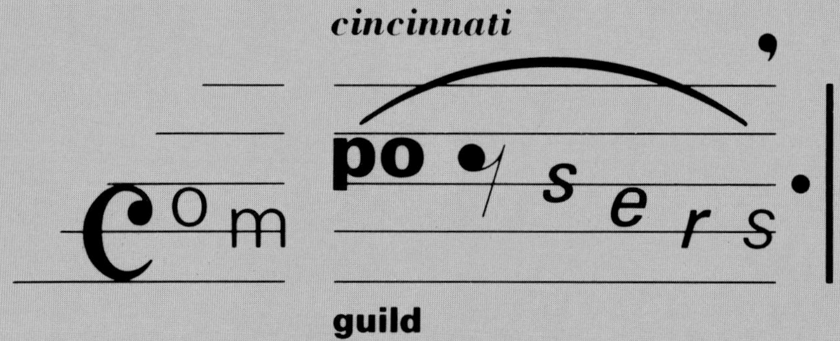

Category:
Logo
Country:
USA
Year Produced:
1983
Art Director:
Jane Kosstrin and David Sterling
Designer:
David Sterling and Jane Kosstrin
Design Firm:
Doublespace
Client:
Union Square Theater and
Queens Theater In The Park

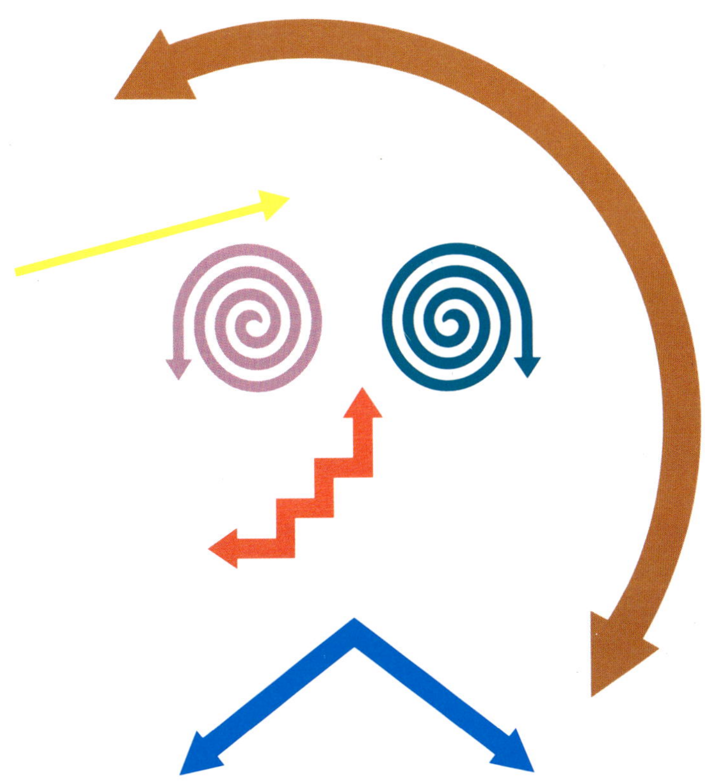

Category:
Logo
Country:
USA
Year Produced:
1987
Art Director:
Mark Palmer
Designer:
Mark Palmer
Design Firm:
Mark Palmer Design
Client:
The Annenberg Center for Health
Sciences at Eisenhower Medical
Center and Canyon Springs Hospital

MIKE SALISBURY
COMMUNICATIONS
2 2 0 0
AMAPOLA
COURT
TORRANCE, CA
9 0 5 0 1

MIKE SALISBURY
COMMUNICATIONS
2 2 0 0
AMAPOLA
COURT
TORRANCE, CA
9 0 5 0 1
213 320-7660

A & M Records
Akadama (WRG)
Baskin-Robbins (DEM)
Blue Note Records
BodyBoarding Magazine
Brittania Jeans (WRG)
Bud Light (Santel)
C & H Sugar (FCB Honig)
Camels (McCann/Erickson)
CBS Fox Video
CBS/Columbia Records
Chastain Shadow
Chevrolet (Vic Olesen)
Chrysler Corp.
City Magazine
Coco's Restaurants (DYR)
Columbia Pictures
Criswell Development Co.
D.E.G.
Disneyland
Dorman Winthrop
Embassy Pictures
Esquire
Fats Domino
Filmex
Frances Coppola
George Harrison
Giorgio
Gordon & Smith
Gotcha
Harper's Bazaar
Harry's Bar & American Grill
Hollywood Reporter
Jack in the Box (WRG)
James Taylor
Jerry Magnin
Keystone Resort (WRG)
Levi Strauss (FCB, Honig)
Life
Lincoln Mercury
London Sunday Times
Lorimar
Los Angeles Herald Examiner
Los Angeles Times
LucasFilm
Made in the Shade Jeans
Mattel Toys (DEM)
Medallion Books
MGM
Michael Jackson
Nalley Foods
National Endowment for the Arts
NBC
New Horizon Pictures
New World Pictures
Newport Publications
Newsweek
O'Neill
Ocean Pacific Sunwear, Ltd.
Orion Pictures
Paramount Pictures
Petersen Publishing
Playboy
Ponderosa Homes
Ralston-Purina (WRG)
Randy Newman
RCA
Revell Toys (DYR)
Rickie Lee Jones
Rolling Stone Magazine
San Francisco Examiner
Schick
Scotti Bros. Records
Sebastian International
Software Ventures
Standard Shoes
StraightArrow Books
Surfing Magazine
Tina Turner
Tri-Star Pictures
Twentieth Century Fox
U.S. Suzuki (DYR)
United Artists
Universal Studios
Vogue
Warner Bros. Pictures
Warner Bros. Records
Warner Home Video
White Water Falls (W.B. Doner)
XEGM AM 95

Category:
Stationery
Country:
USA
Year Produced:
1988
Art Director:
Mike Salisbury
Designer:
Cindy Luck
Design Firm:
Salisbury Communications, Inc.
Client:
Salisbury Communications, Inc.

THIS IS ONLY AN ESTIMATE. FINAL COSTS MAY VARY. THIS PURCHASE ORDER REQUEST DOES NOT INCLUDE USAGE OR REPRODUCTION RIGHTS OF ANY KIND, INCLUDING RETENTION OF ORIGINAL ARTWORK, UNLESS OTHERWISE SPECIFIED. *IF CONCEPTS FROM INITIAL CREATIVE DEVELOPMENT STAGES ARE USED IN ANY FINAL FORM, EVEN THOUGH FINISHED BY OTHERS, A CREATIVE FINISH FEE WILL BE DUE AND PAYABLE.* ANY RIGHTS NOT SO SPECIFIED SHALL BE DEEMED NOT INCLUDED. THIS SUPERCEDES ANY AND ALL OTHER AGREEMENTS UNTIL FINAL BILLING.

1501

INVOICE:
DATE:
OUR JOB #:
YOUR P.O. #:
DUE DATE:

ON PREMISES WORK PAID WITHIN 10 DAYS. VENDORS PAID MONTHLY. ALL OTHER PAID UPON RECEIPT OF CLIENT PAYMENT.

NO INVOICES ARE ACCEPTED WITHOUT A PURCHASE ORDER NUMBER. TO EXPEDITE PAYMENT, PLEASE RETURN A COPY OF THIS FORM AND A COPY OF THE WORK DONE TO:

MIKE SALISBURY COMMUNICATIONS 2200 AMAPOLA CT TORRANCE CA 90501 213 320-7660

DATE:
JOB #:
WRITER:

MIKE SALISBURY COMMUNICATIONS 2200 AMAPOLA CT TORRANCE CA 90501 213 320-7660

Category:
Identity Campaign
Country:
USA
Year Produced:
1988
Art Director:
Mike Salisbury
Designer:
Cindy Luck
Design Firm:
Salisbury Communications, Inc
Client:

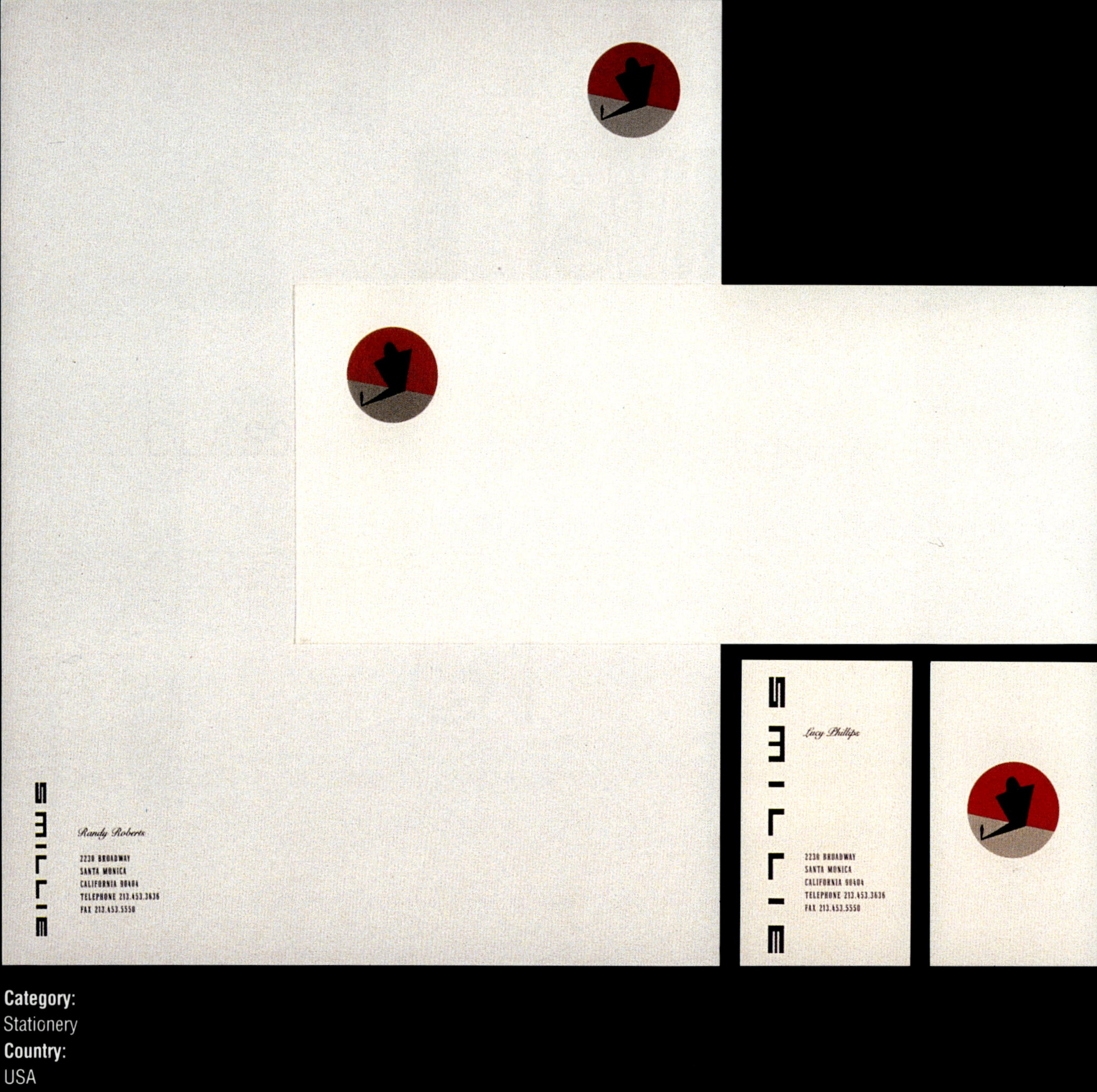

Category:
Stationery
Country:
USA
Year Produced:
1988
Art Director:
Jay Vigon and Rick Seireeni
Designer:
Jay Vigon
Design Firm:
Vigon/Seireeni
Client:
Smillie Productions

Red White & Blue

Productions Inc.

301 West 57th Street,

Suite 49B

New York, NY

10019-3114

Tel: 212 315 5050

Fax: 212 956 8038

Radio Production

•

Video Production

•

Music Production

•

Radio Copywriting

•

Casting

•

SFX & Music

Library

Red White & Blue

Productions Inc.

301 West 57th Street,

Suite 49B

New York, NY

10019-3114

Category:
Logo
Country:
USA
Year Produced:
1989
Art Director:
Courtney Reeser
Designer:
Courtney Reeser
Design Firm:
SBG Partners
Client:
3M Aerospace

Category:
Logo
Country:
Sweden
Year Produced:
1987
Art Director:
Kari Palmqvist
Designer:
Kari Palmqvist
Design Firm:
Studio Bubblan
Client:
Stadsstudie Centrum

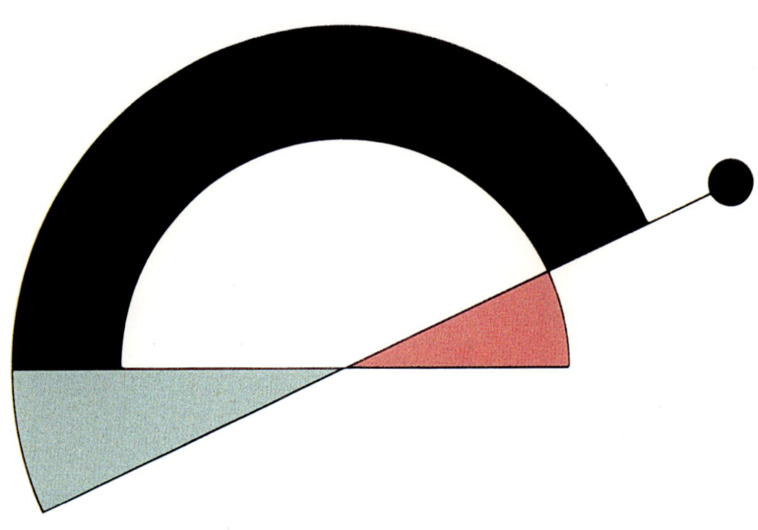

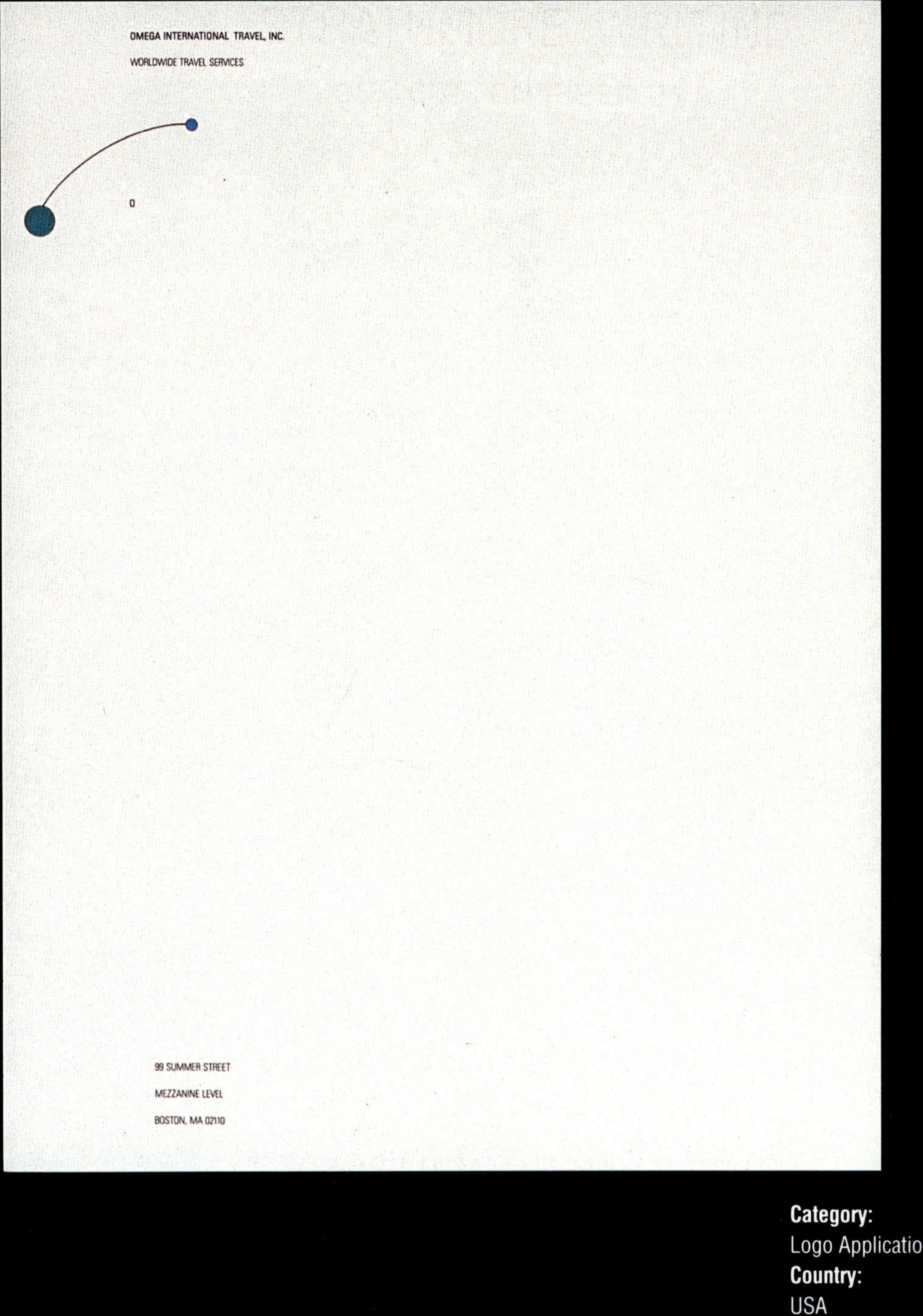

Category:
Logo Application
Country:
USA
Year Produced:
1985
Art Director:
Marc Sawyer
Designer:
Marc Sawyer
Design Firm:
Geneva Design
Client:
Omega International

Category:
Logo
Country:
USA
Year Produced:
1987
Art Director:
Kym Abrams
Designer:
Kym Abrams
Design Firm:
Kym Abrams
Client:
Doctronics

Category:
Logo
Country:
USA
Year Produced:
1986
Art Director:
Rex Peteet and Tom White
Designer:
Rex Peteet
Design Firm:
Sibley/Peteet Design
Client:
Saunders, Lubinsky & White/Lone Star Donuts
Illustrator:
John Evans

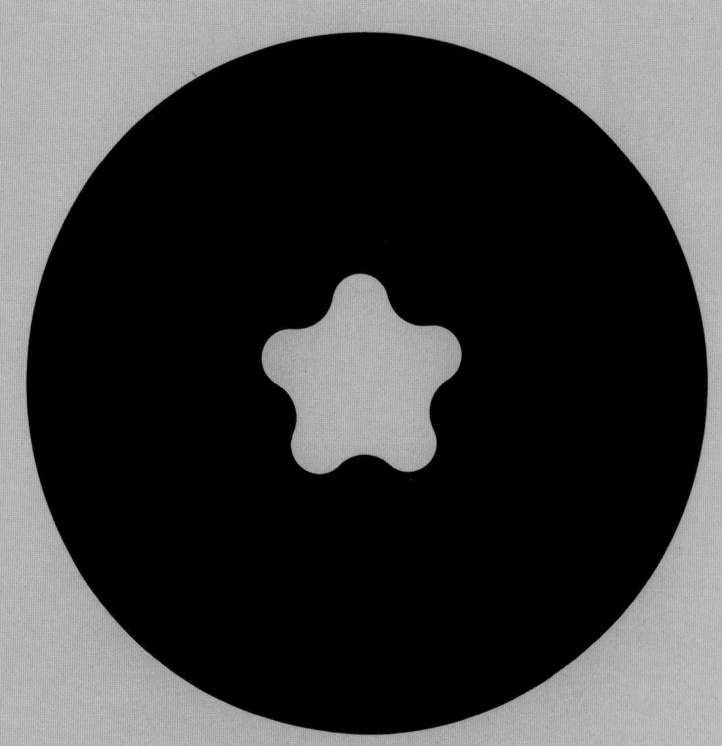

Category:
Logo
Country:
Denmark
Year Produced:
1986
Art Director:
Poul K. Andersen
Designer:
Orn Vidarsson
Design Firm:
Siegel & Gale A/S
Client:
Dane Age

Category:
Logo
Country:
USA
Year Produced:
1989
Art Director:
Robert Rogers
Designer:
Robert Rogers
Design Firm:
IDE, Inc.
Client:
THStyme, Inc.

Category:
Logo
Country:
USA
Year Produced:
1987
Art Director:
John Norman
Designer:
John Norman
Design Firm:
Richards, Brock, Miller, Mitchell & Associates
Client:
Dial-A-Lunch

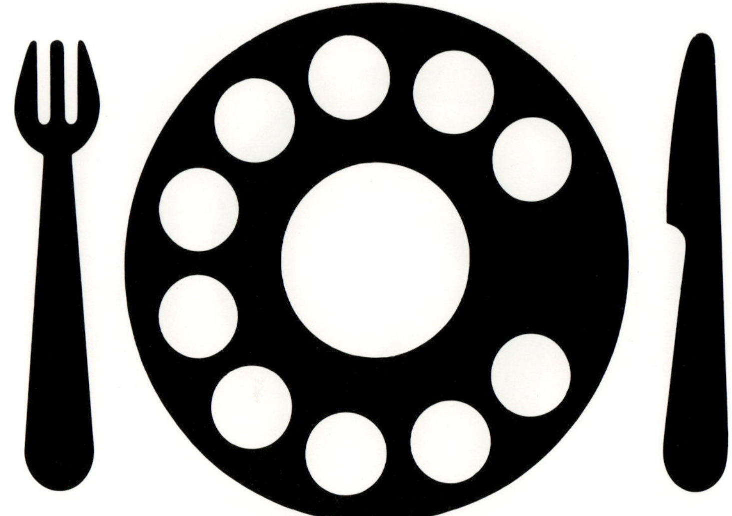

Category:
Logo
Country:
Hong Kong
Year Produced:
1980
Art Director:
Kan Tai-keung
Designer:
Kan Tai-keung and Benjamin Lau
Design Firm:
Kan Tai-keung Design & Associates, Ltd.
Client:
Bank of China

Category:
Logo
Country:
Italy
Year Produced:
1986
Art Director:
Franco Bassi
Designer:
Susanna Crisanti
Design Firm:
Studio 77
Client:
Isefi

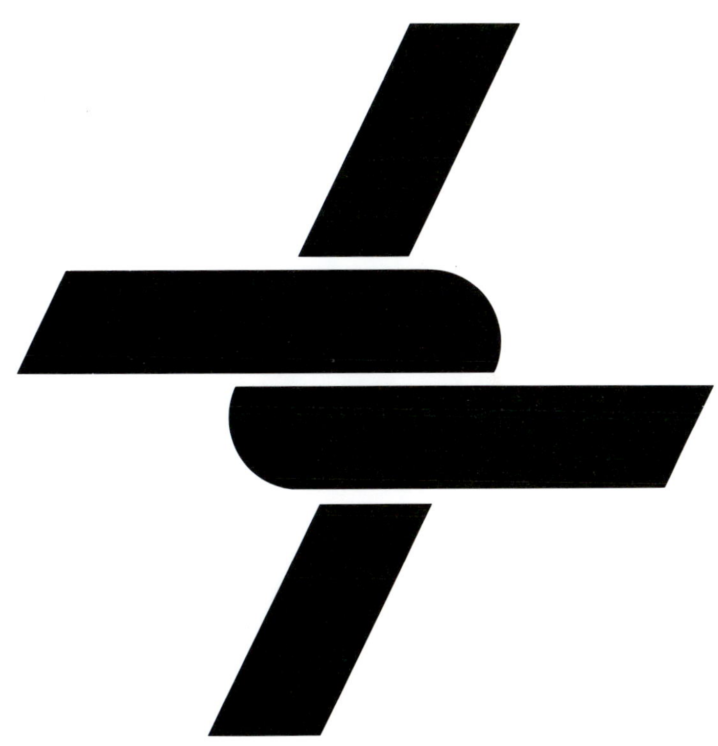

Category:
Logo
Country:
USA
Year Produced:
1984
Art Director:
John Caruso
Designer:
John Caruso
Design Firm:
Sparkman Byrd & Associates, Inc.
Client:
LazerLock United Software Security

Category:
Logo
Country:
New Zealand
Year Produced:
1982
Art Director:
Colin Simon
Designer:
Colin Simon
Design Firm:
Colin Simon Design
Client:
Woollen & Worsted Fabrics, Ltd.

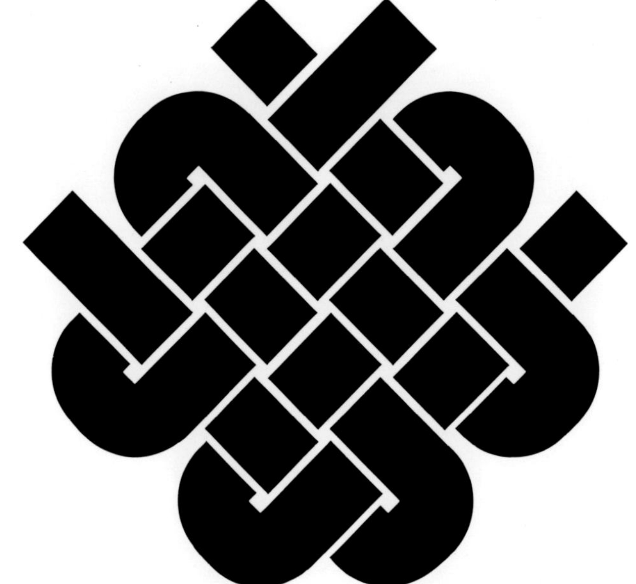

Category:
Logo
Country:
USA
Year Produced:
1984
Art Director:
Jann Church
Designer:
Jann Church
Design Firm:
Jann Church Partners, Advertising & Graphic Design
Client:
Apothecary

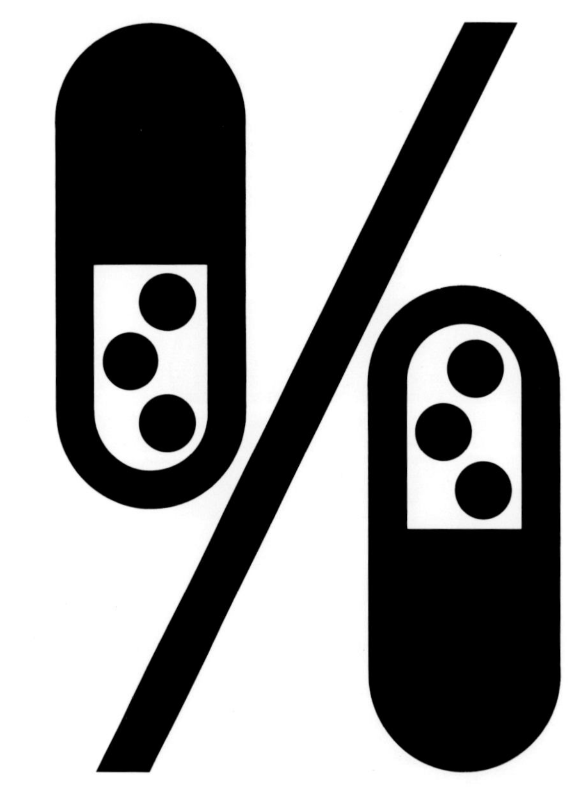

Category:
Logo
Country:
USA
Year Produced:
1985
Art Director:
Dave Kottler
Designer:
Dave Kottler and Paul Caldera
Design Firm:
The Kottler Caldera Group
Client:
MotherWorks, Inc.

Category:
Logo
Country:
USA
Year Produced:
1984
Art Director:
Gerald Gallo
Designer:
Gerald Gallo
Design Firm:
Graphics By Gallo
Client:
The Aluminum Association, Inc.

Category:
Logo
Country:
USA
Year Produced:
1989
Art Director:
David Beck
Designer:
David Beck
Design Firm:
Richards, Brock, Miller, Mitchell & Associates
Client:
ProMotivators

Category:
Logo
Country:
Sweden
Year Produced:
1985
Art Director:
Kari Palmqvist
Designer:
Kari Palmqvist
Design Firm:
Studio Bubblan
Client:
Incite Innovation

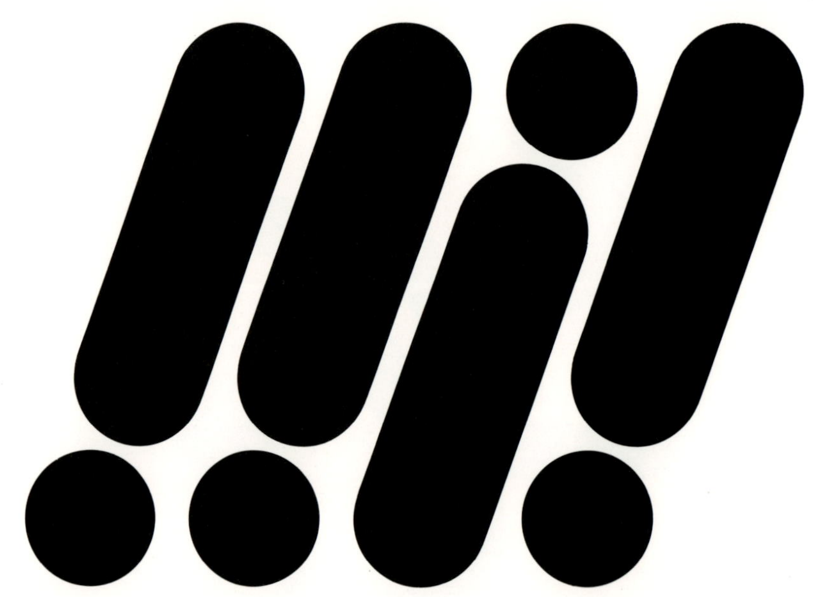

Category:
Logo
Country:
New Zealand
Year Produced:
1980
Art Director:
Colin Simon
Designer:
Colin Simon
Design Firm:
Colin Simon Design
Client:
Colin Simon Design

Category:
Logo
Country:
USA
Year Produced:
1984
Art Director:
Jay Vigon and Rick Seireeni
Designer:
Jay Vigon
Design Firm:
Vigon/Seireeni
Client:
Vigon/Seireeni

Category:
Logo
Country:
USA
Year Produced:
1989
Art Director:
Jay Vigon
Designer:
Jay Vigon
Design Firm:
Jay Vigon
Client:
Jay Vigon

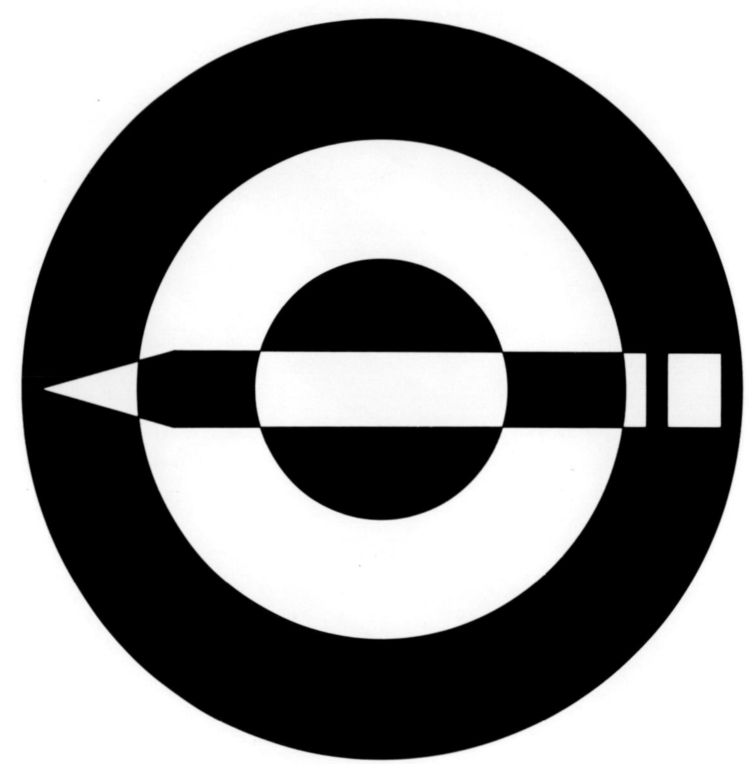

Category:
Logo
Country:
USA
Year Produced:
1989
Art Director:
Giulio Turturro
Designer:
Giulio Turturro
Design Firm:
T & A Design
Client:
Giulio Turturro Graphic Design

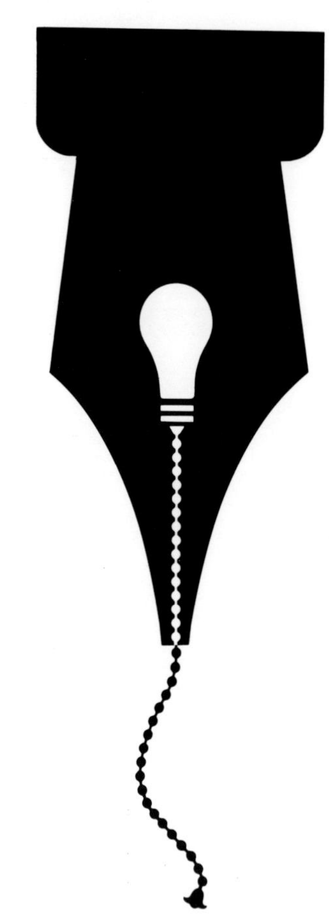

Design and Art Direction

JAY VIGON

11833 Brookdale Lane
Studio City, California 91604
Tel. 213 654 4771 or 654 4996
Fax 213 654 1915

Design and Art Direction

JAY VIGON

11833 Brookdale Lane
Studio City, California 91604
Tel. 213 654 4771 or 654 4996
Fax 213 654 1915

Category:
Stationery
Country:
USA
Year Produced:
1989
Art Director:
Jay Vigon

Category:
Logo
Country:
Japan
Year Produced:
1980
Art Director:
Shigeo Katsuoka
Designer:
Hideaki Shiota
Design Firm:
Shigeo Katsuoka Design Studio
Client:
Nippon Comsys Corporation

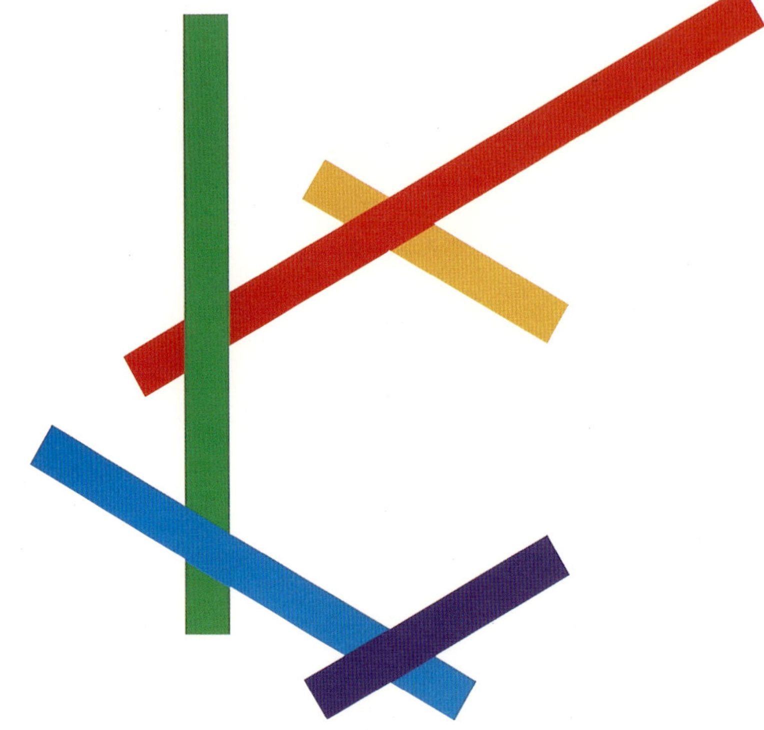

Category:
Logo
Country:
USA
Year Produced:
1989
Art Director:
Planet Design Company
Designer:
Planet Design Company
Design Firm:
Planet Design Company
Client:
Lamop Hair Studio

Category:
Logo Application
Country:
USA
Year Produced:
1989
Art Director:
Keith Bright
Designer:
Il Chung
Design Firm:
Bright & Associates
Client:
Murauchi Furniture Access

Category:
Identity Campaign
Country:
Japan
Year Produced:
1980
Art Director:
Shigeo Katsuoka
Designer:
Hironobu Yamada
Design Firm:
Shigeo Katsuoka Design Studio
Client:
Kyudenko Corporation

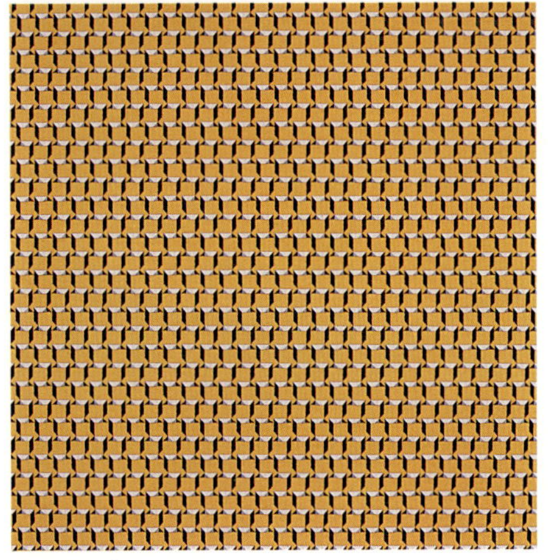

Category:
Identity Campaign
Country:
Poland
Year Produced:
1987
Art Director:
Wlodzimierz Matachowski
Designer:
Wlodzimierz Matachowski
Design Firm:
Wlodzimierz Matachowski
Client:
DSW-Lodz '87

Category:
Packaging
Country:
USA
Year Produced:
1989
Art Director:
Hock W. Yeo
Designer:
Hock W. Yeo
Design Firm:
The Design Office of Wong & Yeo
Client:
Buehler Vineyards
Illustrator:
Lisa Buehler

Category:
Logo Application
Country:
USA
Year Produced:
1989
Art Director:
John Coy
Designer:
John Coy and Laurie Handler
Design Firm:
COY
Client:
South Coast Plaza

Category:
Logo
Country:
Hong Kong
Year Produced:
1988
Art Director:
Freeman Lau Siu-hong
Designer:
Freeman Lau Siu-hong
Design Firm:
Kan Tai-keung Design & Associates, Ltd.
Client:
Freeman Lau Design & Associates, Ltd.

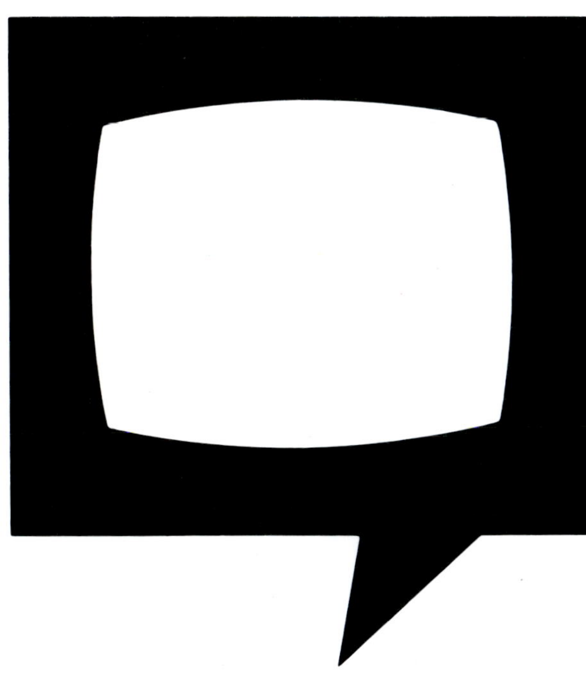

Category:
Logo
Country:
USA
Year Produced:
1980
Art Director:
Philip Gips
Designer:
Philip Gips
Design Firm:
Frankfurt Gips Balkind
Client:
National Captioning Institute

Category:
Logo
Country:
England
Year Produced:
1985
Art Director:
Alan Fletcher
Designer:
Tessa Boo Mitford
Design Firm:
Pentagram
Client:
Mandarin Oriental Hotel Group

Category:
Logo
Country:
Iran
Year Produced:
1986
Art Director:
Morteza Momayez
Designer:
Morteza Momayez
Design Firm:
Momayez's Studio
Client:
Nemoon Publisher Company

Category:
Logo Application
Country:
Japan
Year Produced:
1989
Art Director:
Shin Matsunaga
Designer:
Shin Matsunaga
Design Firm:
Shin Matsunaga Design, Inc.
Client:
ICOGRADA/Japan Graphic Designers Association

Category:
Packaging
Country:
USA
Year Produced:
1989
Art Director:
Patrick Soohoo
Designer:
Paula Yamasaki-Ison, Katherine Lam and Tricia Rauen
Design Firm:
Patrick Soohoo Designers
Client:
Los Angeles County Museum of Art

Category:
Logo Application
Country:
USA
Year Produced:
1988
Art Director:
Marcia Romanuck
Designer:
Denise Pickering and Marcia Romanuck
Design Firm:
The Design Company
Client:
The Design Company

Category:
Logo
Country:
USA
Year Produced:
1987
Art Director:
Cheryl Chung
Designer:
Stefan Sagmeister and Jeanne Greco
Design Firm:
Parham-Santana, Inc.
Client:
Swatch U.S.A.

Category:
Logo
Country:
USA
Year Produced:
1988
Art Director:
Jackson Boelts and Eric Boelts
Designer:
Jackson Boelts, Eric Boelts and
Kerry Stratford
Design Firm:
Boelts Brothers Design, Inc.
Client:
Southwest Traditions, *Home Builder*

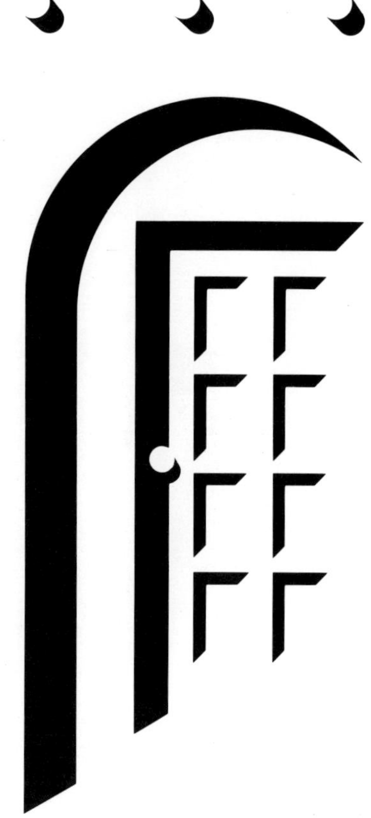

Category:
Logo
Country:
USA
Year Produced:
1987
Art Director:
David Beck
Designer:
David Beck
Design Firm:
Sibley/Peteet Design
Client:
LaSalle Partners

Category:
Logo
Country:
USA
Year Produced:
1989
Art Director:
John Reger
Designer:
Chittamai Suvongse
Design Firm:
Design Center
Client:
Station 19 Architects

Category:
Logo
Country:
USA
Year Produced:
1987
Art Director:
Jerry McPhail, Don Sibley and Rex Peteet
Designer:
Paul Black
Design Firm:
Sibley/Peteet Design
Client:
Crume-Coker/Centex

Category:
Packaging
Country:
Hong Kong
Year Produced:
1988
Art Director:
Kan Tai-keung
Designer:
Kan Tai-keung, Freeman Lau Siu-hong,
Eddy Yu Chi-kong and Clement Yick Tat-wa
Design Firm:
Kan Tai-keung Design & Associates, Ltd.
Client:
Kan Tai-keung Design & Associates, Ltd.

Category:
Logo
Country:
USA
Year Produced:
1986
Art Director:
Lance Wyman
Designer:
Lance Wyman and Christina Walker
Design Firm:
Lance Wyman, Ltd.
Client:
Exchange Place Centre

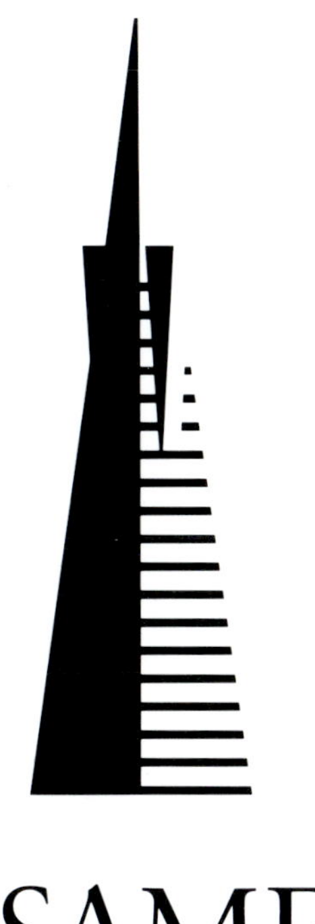

TRANSAMERICA

Category:
Logo
Country:
USA
Year Produced:
1988
Art Director:
Courtney Reeser and Nicolas Sidjakov
Designer:
Thomas Bond
Design Firm:
SBG Partners
Client:
Transamerica Corporation

Category:
Logo
Country:
Japan
Year Produced:
1989
Art Director:
Kijuro Yahagi
Designer:
Kijuro Yahagi
Design Firm:
Kijuro Yahagi Company, Ltd.
Client:
Tokyo Metropolitan Teien Art Museum

Category:
Logo
Country:
USA
Year Produced:
1986
Art Director:
Steven B. Rousso
Designer:
Steven B. Rousso
Design Firm:
Rousso & Associates
Client:
Taylor & Mathis

Category:
Logo
Country:
Lithuania
Year Produced:
1989
Art Director:
Isaak Zibuts
Designer:
Isaak Zibuts
Design Firm:
Jerushalayim De-Lita
Client:
Jewish State Museum of Lithuania

Category:
Logo
Country:
USA
Year Produced:
1985
Art Director:
Landor Associates
Designer:
Landor Associates
Design Firm:
Landor Associates
Client:
Black & Decker

M U R R A Y   C O X   &   A S S O C I A T E S

BUILDING DESIGNERS
& CONSULTANTS
83 MILL POINT ROAD
SOUTH PERTH 6151
WESTERN AUSTRALIA
TELEPHONE 367 9956
TELEX MILL PT
AA94820/CODE 004

Category:
Logo
Country:
Australia
Year Produced:
1982
Art Director:
Rick Lambert
Designer:
Rick Lambert
Design Firm:
Rick Lambert Design Consultants
Client:
Murray Cox & Associates

Category:
Logo
Country:
USA
Year Produced:
1987
Art Director:
Mike Quon and Peter Burke
Designer:
Mike Quon
Design Firm:
Mike Quon Design Office
Client:
Private Satellite Network

Category:
Logo
Country:
USA
Year Produced:
1987
Art Director:
Jack Anderson
Designer:
Jack Anderson and Juliet Shen
Design Firm:
Hornall Anderson Design Works
Client:
Development Services of America

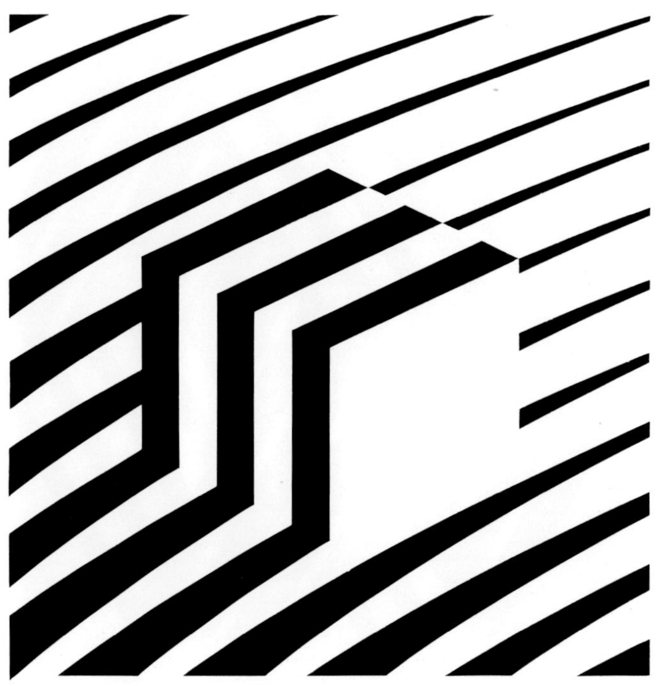

Category:
Logo
Country:
USA
Year Produced:
1981
Art Director:
Ryo Urano
Designer:
Ryo Urano
Design Firm:
Urano Communication International
Client:
Tel-Net Venture Corporation

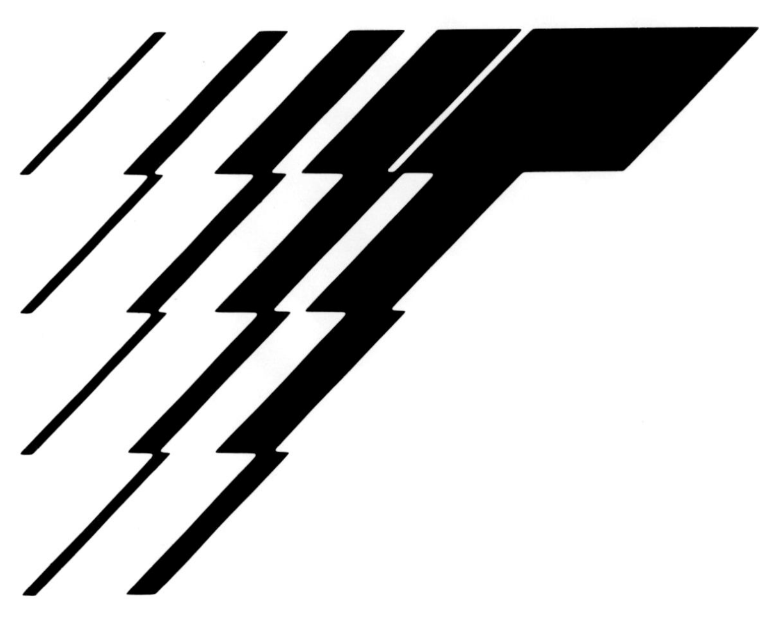

Category:
Logo
Country:
Canada
Year Produced:
1984
Art Director:
Stuart Ash
Designer:
Stuart Ash and George Vaitkunas
Design Firm:
Gottschalk+Ash International
Client:
Rogers Cantel, Inc.

Category:
Logo
Country:
England
Year Produced:
1988
Art Director:
Tor Pettersen
Designer:
Tor Pettersen, Colleen Crim and David C. Brown
Design Firm:
Tor Pettersen & Partners
Client:
Curtin Watson International

Category:
Logo
Country:
USA
Year Produced:
1986
Art Director:
Steven R. Grigg
Designer:
Steven R. Grigg
Design Firm:
Tandem Studios
Client:
Beehive International

Category:
Logo
Country:
USA
Year Produced:
1988
Art Director:
Samuel Kuo
Designer:
Samuel Kuo
Design Firm:
Samuel Kuo Design
Client:
Cereus Software Company

CEREUS

Category:
Logo
Country:
USA
Year Produced:
1989
Art Director:
Tim Thompson
Designer:
Morton Jackson, Joe Parisi and Dave Plunkert
Design Firm:
Graffito
Client:
Graffito

Category:
Logo
Country:
USA
Year Produced:
1989
Art Director:
Craig Butler
Designer:
Jay Vigon
Design Firm:
Butler Design & Jay Vigon
Client:
Scott & Daughters

Category:
Logo
Country:
France
Year Produced:
1988
Art Director:
Cornu-Malcourant
Designer:
Cornu-Malcourant
Design Firm:
Cornu-Malcourant
Client:
Salon des Arts Menagers International

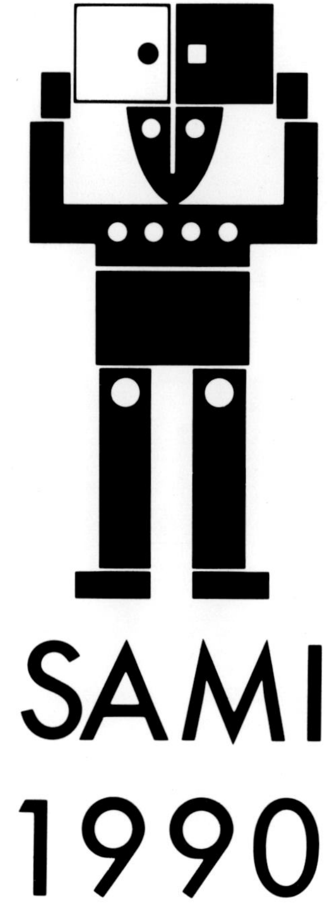

Category:
Logo
Country:
USA
Year Produced:
1984
Art Director:
Jay Vigon and Rick Seireeni
Designer:
Jay Vigon
Design Firm:
Vigon/Seireeni
Client:
Ron Ellison

Category:
Logo
Country:
USA
Year Produced:
1989
Art Director:
Kevin Whaley
Designer:
Kevin Whaley
Design Firm:
Grand Pre' & Whaley, Ltd.
Client:
Chargo Printing

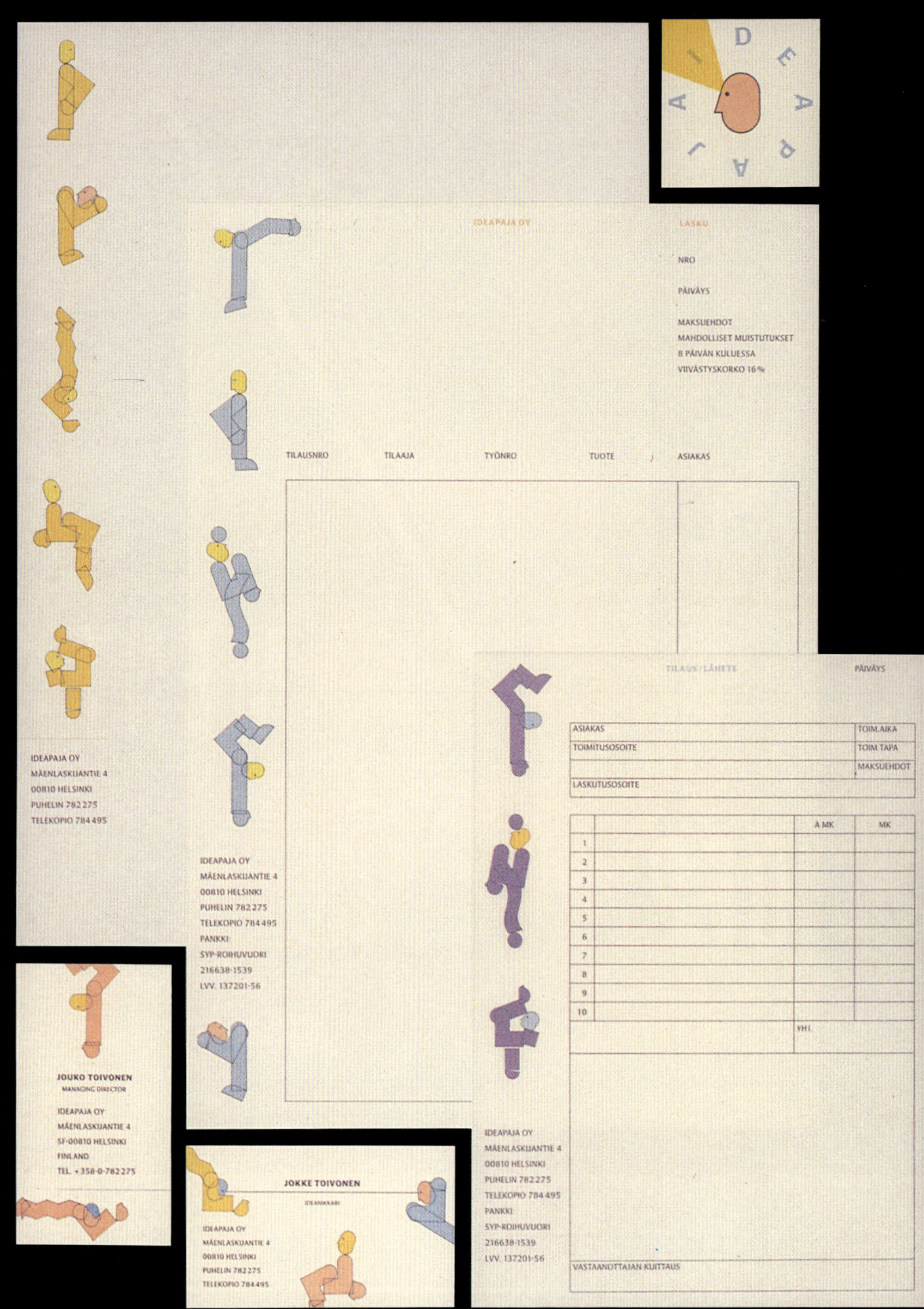

Category:
Identity Campaign
Country:
Finland
Year Produced:
1988
Art Director:
Viktor Kaltala
Designer:
Viktor Kaltala
Design Firm:
Konseph Oy
Client:
Ideapaja Oy

Category:
Stationery
Country:
USA
Year Produced:
1988
Art Director:
Art Kane and Mike Quon
Designer:
Mike Quon and E. Fogarty
Design Firm:
Mike Quon Design Office
Client:
Art Kane Photography

Category:
Packaging
Country:
USA
Year Produced:
1989
Art Director:
Don Sibley and Jim Bremer
Designer:
John Evans
Design Firm:
Sibley/Peteet Design
Client:
Milton Bradley

Category:
Logo
Country:
USA
Year Produced:
1982
Art Director:
Jim Lienhart
Designer:
Jim Lienhart
Design Firm:
Murrie Lienhart Associates
Client:
Continental Bank

Category:
Logo
Country:
Sweden
Year Produced:
1988
Art Director:
Kari Palmqvist
Designer:
Kari Palmqvist
Design Firm:
Studio Bubblan
Client:
Kontorsutveckling/Esselte

Category:
Stationery
Country:
USA
Year Produced:
1985
Art Director:
Keith Bright
Designer:
Peter Sargent and Wilson Ong
Design Firm:
Bright & Associates
Client:
Andresen Typographics, Inc.

Category:
Logo
Country:
USA
Year Produced:
1987
Art Director:
Ryo Urano
Designer:
Dan Sato
Design Firm:
Urano Communication International
Client:
Yoshida Kinen Tennis
Training Center

Category:
Logo
Country:
USA
Year Produced:
1987
Art Director:
Lance Wyman
Designer:
Lance Wyman and Christina Walker
Design Firm:
Lance Wyman, Ltd.
Client:
USTA National Tennis Center

Category:
Logo
Country:
USA
Year Produced:
1982
Art Director:
Sachi Kuwahara
Designer:
Sachi Kuwahara
Design Firm:
Sawcheese Studio
Client:
Sawcheese Studio

Category:
Logo
Country:
USA
Year Produced:
1982
Art Director:
Mitch Lindgren
Designer:
Mitch Lindgren
Design Firm:
Pedersen & Gesk, Inc.
Client:
WCCO-TV

Category:
Logo
Country:
USA
Year Produced:
1988
Art Director:
Don Weller, Mikio Osaki and Jon Anderson
Designer:
Don Weller
Design Firm:
The Weller Institute for the Cure of Design, Inc.
Client:
The Design Conference That Just Happens To Be In Park City

Category:
Logo
Country:
USA
Year Produced:
1980
Art Director:
John Reger
Designer:
John Reger
Design Firm:
Design Center
Client:
3M Companies

C L I E N T

CLIENT

ART DIRECTOR

DESIGNER

DESIGN FIRM